Reading Wonders
Food for Thought and Communication

Robert Juppe   Yukio Umaba

KINSEIDO

Kinseido Publishing Co., Ltd.
3-21 Kanda Jimbo-cho, Chiyoda-ku,
Tokyo 101-0051, Japan

Copyright © 2015 by Robert Juppe
　　　　　　　　　Yukio Umaba

All rights reserved. No part of this publication may be reproduced, stored in a retrieval system, or transmitted, in any form or by any means, electronic, mechanical, photocopying, recording or otherwise, without the prior permission of the publisher.

First published 2015 by Kinseido Publishing Co., Ltd.

Cover design　Takayuki Minegishi
Text design　　guild
Illustrations　　Yuko Saito

Acknowledgement
Photos　　　Unit 9　AFP= 時事
　　　　　　Unit 10　AFP= 時事

音声ファイル無料ダウンロード

http://www.kinsei-do.co.jp/download/3999

この教科書で　DL 00 の表示がある箇所の音声は、上記 URL または QR コードにて無料でダウンロードできます。自習用音声としてご活用ください。

▶ PC からのダウンロードをお勧めします。スマートフォンなどでダウンロードされる場合は、
　ダウンロード前に「解凍アプリ」をインストールしてください。
▶ URL は、検索ボックスではなくアドレスバー (URL 表示覧) に入力してください。
▶ お使いのネットワーク環境によっては、ダウンロードできない場合があります。

CD 00　左記の表示がある箇所の音声は、教室用 CD（Class Audio CD）に収録されています。

はしがき

　この本の表紙をご覧下さい。手に取ったときどう思われましたか。アメリカ中西部の風景でしょうか。皆さんは今手前の道に立っています。皆さんが目指すのは大きな木のずっと向こう側ですね。今よりも英語の力がついた世界へ皆さんを少しでも導ければと願って、この本を2人で作りました。上級者向けの教材ということで、本文の英文の量だけでなく、付随する練習問題の量も多くしてあります。

　現代は机上にあるコンピューターではなく、持ち運びの出来る携帯やパソコンで何でも検索できる、また他国の人とも瞬時にメールや電話で交流がはかれるグローバルな時代といえます。英語をもっと「話す」「書く」に重点を置くコミュニケーション重視の英語教育の流れも当然といえます。しかし、上級者の皆さんはご存じのように、この2つの技能を伸ばすには、英語を「読む」「聞く」量を格段と増やす必要があります。本書はまさにこのために作られたものといえます。

　この本の構成は簡単なものにしてあります。**VOCABULARY PREVIEW** では本文を理解する上で大事な単語を読む前に確認します。**READING** は本文の右に単語の意味を書いておきましたが、数は最小限に抑えてあります。単語の意味をその前後関係から類推する力を奪いたくないからです。そのあと内容理解のための **COMPREHENSION**、そして要約文作成のための **SUMMARY** へと進みます。次に本文題材に関するテーマを **DIALOGUE** 形式で聞き、又は読み、更にこの **COMPREHENSION** もつけてあります。最後の **VOCABULARY BUILDING** では2種類のタスクを通して、本文、テーマに沿った語・語句の確認を行います。時間に応じて取捨選択してもらってもかまわないと思います。

　皆さんには大量の英語を「読む」「聞く」ことで、英語の語感を是非つけて頂きたいと思います。副題の **Food for Thought and Communication** とは「思考、コミュニケーションへの糧」という意味です。皆さんには英語が単に話せるだけではなく、内容のあることを話せる人に是非なってほしいと願います。英語上達への道は時間がかかることを皆さんはご存じだとは思います。時にはこの大木の木陰で休むことも必要でしょうが、あきらめずにこの彼方を目指してもらえたらと思います。さあ、まず第一歩から進みましょう。

著　者

Contents

Unit	Title	Page
1	A Snowman That Neither Melted Nor Stuck	1
2	The Secret Test Pilot	7
3	The Pub, an Endangered British Species	13
4	Sleep Habits in the Mammal Kingdom	19
5	The Secret Behind the Image	25
6	The Periodic Cicada, an Amazing Survivor	31
7	The Story Behind a Modern Wonder Drug	37
8	Black Friday	43
9	Getting High on Gardening	49
10	The Throw-Away Café!	55
11	Lost in Translation?	61
12	The Very Fortunate Four	67
13	Health, a Salty Reality	73
14	First the Mammoth, Next the Elephant?	79
15	Battling the Blues	85

Unit 1
A Snowman That Neither Melted Nor Stuck

馬というと多くの人はその美しい毛並み、優しそうな目を挙げる人が多いと思います。昔は馬は人間にとって現代の車のような交通手段であり、農作業には欠かせない動物でもあったのです。しかし、現代では競馬場や乗馬教室ぐらいでしか見かけなくなってしまいました。そんな馬たちも、悲しいことですが、価値がなくなると解体場に送られ、肉の一部が売られたりするわけです。この課ではスノーマンという非常に運に恵まれたある馬の話を読んでみましょう。

✲ VOCABULARY PREVIEW

次の空欄にあてはまる適切な語を a ～ c から選びましょう。

1. Celine is often happy one moment and then angry the next without a good reason. I like her very much, but she is difficult to deal with because she is so _____.
    a. magnificent　　　**b.** moody　　　**c.** moral
2. When you shop at a flea market, prices are not fixed. You have to _____ with the shop owners before a price is agreed upon.
    a. negotiate　　　**b.** nominate　　　**c.** navigate
3. My parents hate everything I do, especially my mother. She is always _____ of my friends, my clothing, and my lifestyle.
    a. cooperative　　　**b.** confident　　　**c.** critical
4. I _____ much in my life. For example, I am sorry that I did not study more when I was in high school.
    a. rejoice　　　**b.** regret　　　**c.** recruit
5. A dog barks and a cat mews, but a horse _____ when it makes a sound.
    a. neighs　　　**b.** nods　　　**c.** nuzzles

READING

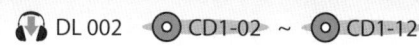

Notes

One snowy afternoon, Harry de Leyer went to an auction. He returned home with a horse he had bought for $80. The horse was thin, weak, and lonely looking. Harry's children ran outside to see their father's latest purchase. Heavy snow had piled up high on the horse's back. Harry's son commented that the animal looked like a snowman. That became the horse's name.

In fact, because of heavy snow on the roads, Harry had been late for the auction. Snowman had been a last minute choice, one of the leftovers. His owners had been leading him away with the other unsold animals just as Harry decided to buy him.

Because Snowman was slower than Harry had expected, he decided to use the new horse in his riding school. Within weeks, Snowman became everyone's favorite horse at the school. He had a pleasant character, never trying to bring riders back to the stable or throw them off. He was just the type of horse that Harry had wanted for his students. Horses could be moody, but Snowman warmed up to everyone.

The school, though, was not doing well at all; Harry decided to close it down. A man who lived nearby offered Harry $200 for Snowman. Harry did not want to give up the horse, as he had grown fond of him, but he needed the money. The man handed Harry $200 in cash and Snowman vanished.

Harry regretted what he had done. His children, too, criticized him for getting rid of the beloved horse. Oddly enough, Harry and his children were not the only ones sorry about the deal. On the first night at his new owner's farm, Snowman jumped over the barnyard fence and escaped. In the morning, Harry found Snowman in his yard. The horse neighed happily when he saw his friend Harry. Harry had to return the horse to its new owner,

auction「競売」

leftover「残り物」

unsold「売れない」

stable「馬小屋」

warm up to「友好的である」

grow fond of ~「~が好きになる」

get rid of ~「~を追い出す」
beloved horse「愛されている馬」

barnyard fence「納屋の柵」

2

however.

The new owner put Snowman in a pen with a higher fence. Again, however, that night the horse leaped over the fence and returned to Harry. Finally, the new owner put up very high fences that would be impossible for a horse to get over. Yet again, the next morning, when Harry came out of his house, there was Snowman.

Harry negotiated; the new owner happily accepted his $200 back in exchange for the horse. Immediately, Harry got to work testing Snowman and found that his hunch had been correct. When he bought Snowman, Harry hoped that he might become a race horse. He discovered that Snowman was not fast, but he could jump. Harry trained him regularly.

By 1959, Snowman had won the greatest prize a horse could hope to receive. 13,000 people applauded loudly at Madison Square Garden in New York when Snowman got his award as "Horse of the Year."

From the age of seven in 1956, Snowman kept winning competitions over the next decade. He lived a long life, dying peacefully in 1969. It was very fortunate that Harry had gotten the chance to discover Snowman's true talent.

There had been seven horses at the auction that snowy day in the early 1950s. Later that day, all of them were sold to a glue factory. They were dead by the end of that week.

Snowman would have been one of them. Thanks to Harry, however, this special horse with a gentle character went on to become one of the most famous horses in history rather than the contents of a bottle of glue.

✻ COMPREHENSION

英文の内容に関する質問の答えとして適切なものを a ～ c から選びましょう。

1. Which of the following is true about Snowman?
    a. He had once been a champion race horse.
    b. He was moody with riding school students.
    c. He nearly died young in the early 1950s.
2. Who gave Snowman his name?
    a. His trainer.   b. Harry's son.   c. An auctioneer.
3. How did Harry de Leyer discover Snowman's talent?
    a. Snowman always returned to Harry after he had been sold.
    b. Snowman outran every horse in important racing competitions.
    c. Harry's son had trained the horse to run in snowy weather.
4. How much "profit" did Harry make when he sold Snowman?
    a. $80.   b. $120.   c. $200.
5. For which of the following did Snowman become famous?
    a. He won a prestigious prize at a horse show in New York City.
    b. He was the most popular horse at Harry's riding school.
    c. His picture was used on a famous brand of glue.

✻ SUMMARY

DL 003   CD1-13

次の（　）内に、与えられた文字で始まる適切な語を1語ずつ入れ、音声を聞いて確認しましょう。

　Snowman is one of the best-known horses of all time, though he was nearly taken away to a ①(g　　　) factory and killed at a very young age. Luckily, Harry de Leyer was able to buy him for a low price at an ②(a　　　).

　Snowman got his name from Harry's son. When the boy first saw the horse, lots of snow had ③(p　　　) up on his back. Snowman fit in well at Harry's riding school because he was not ④(m　　　) with riders.

　Snowman's special ability was discovered after a man living nearby had ⑤(p　　　) the horse from Harry. Though Harry ⑥(r　　　) that he had sold him, Snowman returned to him again and again. He always jumped over the high ⑦(f　　　) put up to keep him in. Harry then ⑧(n　　　) with the new ⑨(o　　　), and soon bought Snowman back for the original sale price.

　Snowman won many ⑩(a　　　) thanks to Harry's hard training.

DIALOGUE

次の会話の音声を聞いて、（　）内に1語ずついれましょう。

（Theo と Rolinda は夕食後に新聞を読んでいます）

R: Theo, this is so interesting! Did you know that Seabiscuit got more print space in newspapers in the United States in 1938 than the president did?

T: Wait a second, Rolinda, who or what is Seabiscuit?

R: Seabiscuit was probably the most ①(　　　　) ②(　　　　) horse of all time. He won ten major races, including the Santa Anita Handicap.

T: OK, he won a lot of races, but what was so special about him?

R: He was a fighter. Though he was small, he had a great spirit. He ③(　　　　) a horse called War Admiral in 1938. War Admiral outweighed Seabiscuit by a lot.

T: So what you are saying is that this is like boxing. The ④(　　　　) the opponent, the better the chances of winning?

R: He was heavily ⑤(　　　　) to lose the race. It is said that 40,000,000 Americans listened to the race on radio.

T: Wow, that was probably about ⑥(　　) ⑦(　　　　) ⑧(　　　) the population.

R: No, Theo, it was a bit more than half of the population. I wish I could have seen that race. It must have been so ⑨(　　　　).

T: I think this movie is at the DVD rental shop near the station. Why don't we rent it tomorrow night? I'm really interested in his story now.

Notes▸ print space「記事の欄」

✲ COMPREHENSION

上の Dialogue の内容に関する質問の答えとして適切なものを a～c から選びましょう。

1. What was special about Seabiscuit?
    a. He ran away from his owner by jumping over fences.
    b. Though he was small, he won many big races.
    c. He was the president's favorite horse at the time.
2. About how many people lived in the United States in 1940?
    a. 40,000,000.　　　b. 80,000,000.　　　c. 160,000,000.

Unit **1**　A Snowman That Neither Melted Nor Stuck

✳✴✳ VOCABULARY BUILDING

A 次の太字の語が同じ対比を表すように、空欄に入る適切な語をa～cから選びましょう。

1. **Horse** is to **glue** as **cow** is to _____.
   a. farm   **b.** bag   **c.** pillow
2. **Stable** is to **horse** as _____ is to **criminal**.
   a. crime   **b.** detective   **c.** prison
3. **Lion** is to **cat** as **zebra** is to _____.
   a. dog   **b.** Africa   **c.** horse
4. **Decade** is to **ten** as _____ is to one **hundred**.
   a. millennium   **b.** year   **c.** century
5. **Negotiate** is to **deal** as _____ is to **competition**.
   a. train   **b.** victory   **c.** prize

B 次の例にならって、空欄にあてはまる適切な語をa～cから選びましょう。

例: When a horse makes a sound, it ___b.___.
   a. mews   **b.** neighs   **c.** roars

1. When a goat makes a sound, it _____.
   a. barks   **b.** purrs   **c.** bleats
2. When a cow makes a sound, it _____.
   a. cackles   **b.** moos   **c.** bellows
3. When a mouse makes a sound, it _____.
   a. squeaks   **b.** roars   **c.** crows
4. When a lion makes a sound, it _____.
   a. mews   **b.** roars   **c.** chirps
5. When a wolf makes a sound, it _____
   a. chirps   **b.** barks   **c.** howls

Unit 2 The Secret Test Pilot

　偉大な発明家の陰には偉大な女性ありとはよく言われます。この課に登場する発明家は完璧主義者で、自分の発明品が自分自身にとって完璧と思えるまでは公表しなかったのです。しかし、彼の妻はそのようには考えなかったのです。彼の妻のおかげで、夫は誰もが知る会社を設立することになったのです。彼の名は？いくつかヒントを差し上げましょう。車、ドイツ、高級車…さて誰でしょう。

✳ VOCABULARY PREVIEW

次の空欄にあてはまる適切な語を a〜c から選びましょう。

1. Though many think that the Internet is the greatest modern _____, it seems to have accomplished little more than speed up communication between people and make access to information much easier.
   a. barrier　　　　**b.** invention　　　　**c.** superstition

2. Yuki faced many hardships in starting his new business. One such _____ was getting a loan.
   a. obstacle　　　　**b.** pleasure　　　　**c.** temptation

3. If you do not want someone to steal your idea for a new product, it is wise to get a _____ from the government.
   a. breakthrough　　　　**b.** device　　　　**c.** patent

4. Except for the wealthier citizens, most people in society have been _____ by the sharp and unfair rise in the consumption tax.
   a. overjoyed　　　　**b.** invested　　　　**c.** plagued

5. I had to get off my bicycle and walk up the mountain while pushing it. The slope was very _____.
   a. steep　　　　**b.** pleasant　　　　**c.** brilliant

READING

In the countryside city of Mannheim, Germany, a brilliant inventor and industrialist was busy with something exciting in the summer of 1888. Karl, as he was known to his friends, had created a three-wheeled wooden vehicle, something like a motorized tricycle. He hoped that this invention would replace the horse and carriage. Many, however, found the thought of this difficult to imagine.

Karl's wife, Bertha, believed otherwise. On the morning of August 5, 1888, unknown to Karl, she had plans for her husband's invention. Bertha slipped out of bed just before sunrise and awoke her two teenage sons. Quietly, they snuck into the workshop behind their home and pushed out her husband's simple-looking horseless carriage.

This *Motorwagen*, for which Karl had already obtained a patent, had no roof, no hood, and naturally, no horse. It had two large wheels in the back and a small one in the front. It had a long handle instead of a wheel for steering. It also had a single-cylinder, gas-powered 2.5 horsepower engine. Karl was not ready to show it to the public; he believed it needed further improvements. His wife, however, was eager to prove that the world was ready for this useful, reliable invention.

The mother and sons left from southwestern Germany and headed for a small town in the Black Forest. Their goal was to reach the mother's birthplace and then return home… a round-trip distance of approximately 110 kilometers.

This first long automobile trip came up against numerous obstacles. For example, the engine had to be cooled. As there was just a single driver's seat and a small bench on which the sons were to sit, bringing water along was impossible. Instead, the sons collected it from puddles and village wells along the way. This had to be done several times.

Moreover, the three had not anticipated problems related to the vehicle's basic parts. The brakes, for instance, were not strong enough yet. The lining on the brake pads quickly wore down. The three found a shoemaker, who nailed pieces of strong leather to the brake blocks. The chains, too, which were similar to modern bicycle chains, were too weak for some of the hills. After the chains broke in several places, Bertha searched for a blacksmith in a village. She found one, and he repaired the chains. Finally, toward the end of their trip, they ran into a problem that would plague drivers for years to come: They ran out of gasoline. There were no gasoline stations, so the boys went to a pharmacy and bought the store's entire supply of stain remover, which amounted to about two liters of liquid. Fortunately, it worked. (That pharmacy is famous today as the world's first automobile filling station, by the way.)

As the sun went down, the three faced one last barrier. Near their home, there was a hill that was too steep to climb. With the help of a farmer who was out in his field working, the two sons pushed the car and their mother to the top, and the team was able to return by dark.

The trip was called a breakthrough. News of the event quickly spread throughout Europe. Though superior automobile models were to appear in the years after, Bertha and her sons had proved that a car was convenient and useful for people. Her husband, too, went on to design other automobiles bearing his name, one that is still known well today: Benz.

Notes

puddle「水たまり」

lining「ライニング（摩擦材）」
brake pad「ブレーキパッド（ディスクブレーキのディスクに押しつけられるパッド）」
wear down「すり減る」
brake block「ブレーキブロック」

run into~「～にぶつかる」
for years to come「これから何年間にもわたって」

pharmacy「薬局」
stain remover「しみ抜き」

breakthrough「画期的成功」

were to「～になっていた（予定を表す）」

bearing his name「彼の名を取って」

✳ COMPREHENSION

英文の内容に関する質問の答えとして適切なものを a～c から選びましょう。

1. Who was the test pilot for the first vehicle made by Karl Benz?
   a. Karl's friend.   b. Karl's son.   c. Karl's spouse.
2. Why did Bertha not wake up her husband on August 5, 1888?
   a. Karl did not want to test the car before it was perfect.
   b. Karl did not want Bertha driving because she had no license.
   c. Karl worried that the brakes might not stop the car.
3. Who helped the team with their final problem, or obstacle?
   a. A blacksmith.   b. A farmer.   c. A pharmacist.
4. How did the group get water to cool the engine?
   a. Thanks to the rain falling that day, there was no need to get water.
   b. They kept containers of water on the bench behind the driver.
   c. They used rainwater from the ground and water from local wells.
5. Which of the following did the group experience on their trip?
   a. The battery ran out of power and needed to be re-charged at a pharmacy.
   b. One of the tires went flat, so the group asked a blacksmith to repair it.
   c. The material on their brakes became thin, so a cobbler had to replace it.

✳ SUMMARY

DL 006   CD1-23

次の（　）内に、与えられた文字で始まる適切な語を1語ずつ入れ、音声を聞いて確認しましょう。

　　Though Karl Benz had [1](i　　　　) a three-wheeled, gasoline-powered [2](v　　　　) by 1888, he hesitated to show it to the public. His adventurous and spirited wife, however, believed that his "car" would be something good for society. She was sure that it would replace the [3](h　　　　) and carriage.

　　She and her two sons [4](s　　　　) into her husband's workshop one morning that summer. Without any water, they headed out on a 110-kilometer trip to Bertha Benz's [5](b　　　　) in the Black Forest. Along the way, they met many [6](o　　　　). For example, they frequently ran out of water. They ran out of gasoline as well. Because there were no filling stations, they bought stain remover at a [7](p　　　　). A blacksmith fixed their chains, which had [8](b　　　　), and a shoemaker repaired their [9](b　　　　).

　　Bertha's trip had been a big [10](b　　　　). The news spread all over Europe.

DIALOGUE

次の会話の音声を聞いて、（　）内に1語ずついれましょう。

(Theo と Rolinda は夕食後に読書をしています)

R: Theo, Amelia Earhart was really a female pioneer, wasn't she? She accomplished so much in her short life as an ①(　　　). For example, she was the first woman to fly across the Atlantic Ocean ②(　　　).

T: Wait a minute … I thought Charles Lindbergh did that.

R: Theo! Was he a WOMAN? Anyway, she was the first person to fly across the ③(　　　) twice, the first woman to fly non-stop across the U.S. from coast to coast, and she achieved many speed records.

T: She did that all in the 1930s, right?

R: She got her pilot's license in 1922, but did not ④(　　　) ⑤(　　　) until she crossed the Atlantic in … let's see … 1927!

T: What a tough life she must have had. You are right, she really was a pioneer.

R: Her life ended so tragically, too. She had finished 22,000 miles of a 29,000 mile trip around the world. She started her ⑥(　　　) ⑦(　　　), which began with an 18-hour trip to Howland Island.

T: Wait…I have heard about this. For two weeks, the U.S. navy searched for her all over the Pacific Ocean, but nothing was ever found.

R: Right! Here, Theo, I'll ⑧(　　　) you this book.

Notes ▸ Howland Island「ハウランド島（太平洋中部の Phoenix 諸島の北西にある島。米国の飛行場がある）」

✱ COMPREHENSION

上の Dialogue の内容に関する質問の答えとして適切なものを a ～ c から選びましょう。

1. For which of the following is Amelia Earhart famous?
   a. She was the first woman in the world to obtain a pilot's license.
   b. She discovered Howland Island while flying across the Pacific.
   c. She flew from coast to coast in the U.S. without stopping.

2. After getting her pilot's license, how long was it before she crossed the Atlantic Ocean?
   a. Two years.　　　b. Five years.　　　c. Eighteen years.

✳✳✳ VOCABULARY BUILDING

A 次の太字の語が同じ対比を表すように、空欄に入る適切な語を a〜c から選びましょう。

1. **Tricycle** is to **three** as _____ is to **one**.
   a. bicycle **b.** automobile **c.** unicycle
2. **Sunset** is to **darkness** as **nursery school** is to _____.
   a. education **b.** invention **c.** obstacle
3. **Obstacle** is to **barrier** as _____ is to **fix**.
   a. quick **b.** repair **c.** succeed
4. **Patent** is to **invention** as _____ is to **manuscript**.
   a. copyright **b.** contract **c.** constitution
5. _____ is to **plane** as **driver** is to **car**.
   a. flight **b.** radium **c.** aviator
6. **Accelerator** is to **go** as _____ is to **stop**.
   a. chain **b.** gasoline **c.** brake

B 受動態を含んだ文です。次の空欄にあてはまる適切な語を a〜c から選びましょう。

1. The telephone was _____ by Alexander Graham Bell.
   a. founded **b.** invented **c.** discovered
2. The theory of relativity was _____ by Albert Einstein.
   a. created **b.** discovered **c.** drawn
3. Transatlantic flights were _____ by Pan American Airlines.
   a. discovered **b.** initiated **c.** filmed
4. The iPod was _____ by Apple.
   a. directed **b.** discovered **c.** developed
5. *Tokyo Story* was _____ by Yasujiro Ozu.
   a. acted **b.** sung **c.** directed

Unit 3 The Pub, an Endangered British Species

英国のパブへ行ったことはありますか？地域の人達が会合で使ったり、ダーツの試合をしたり、1パイントのビールを飲みながらおしゃべりをしたりという、バーとはちょっと違う場所なのです。押し寄せるグローバリゼーションのもと、パブも存続の危機にさらされているのです。英国の人々は将来どこで皆に会うのでしょうか。お互いに隣近所の人を知り合うこともなくなるのでしょうか。パブの存在を脅かしているものは何なのでしょうか。

✻ VOCABULARY PREVIEW

次の空欄にあてはまる適切な語を a ～ c から選びましょう。

1. A(n) _____ tax is paid when a person buys a product or service.
   a. income **b.** consumption **c.** estate
2. After government _____ took place, airline companies were free to set the prices of airline tickets.
   a. deregulation **b.** assistance **c.** support
3. Smoking has been banned in many eating and drinking _____ such as restaurants, shops, and malls.
   a. habits **b.** vehicles **c.** establishments
4. Due to the widespread use of cell phones and other devices, many believe that face-to-face _____ has decreased heavily.
   a. socialization **b.** traffic **c.** revolution
5. My favorite _____ is orange juice. I drink a liter a day.
   a. beverage **b.** obstacle **c.** immigration

13

READING

One might find it surprising to come across a charming old pub, or public house, on a city street in Britain, and then look up to see "Since 1482." One could imagine that such drinking establishments were already old when Francis Bacon or Isaac Newton stopped by for a pint of beer. Pubs have been at the heart of many neighborhoods and towns in Britain for ages.

Pubs have been more than just places to drink alcoholic beverages. They have served as substitute British living rooms for centuries. The pub has been a magnet for people to come together socially. Moreover, pubs have, since long ago, attracted customers with a wide range of ages. This means that socialization takes place between people of different age groups. One could say that pubs often serve as community social centers.

The age of globalization, however, has put the pub in a dangerous position, along with uncountable institutions, habits, and creatures. The number of pubs in England, for example, has declined by 7000 since 2008. This has left some small communities in an unthinkable situation: life without a "local," as pubs are often called. This decline is certain to increase, too.

Beer has always been the most popular beverage in pubs, so changing consumption patterns of the drink are one reason for the decline. Firstly, compared with 2004, people in 2014 drank 23% less beer, according to the British Beer and Pub Association. Health considerations and other beverage options are given as the main reasons for this. Secondly, sales of beer at large discount stores have increased sharply. Younger generations seem to prefer buying inexpensive beer and drinking at home. Finally, immigration seems to have played a part in people's changing tastes. Many of those who have come to England in the past two or three decades come

Notes

come across~「~に出くわす」

look up to see =look up and see

stop by~「~に立ち寄る」

a pint of beer「1 パイント (0.473 リットル) のビール」

magnet「引きつけるもの」

by 7000「7000 も (by で数量・程度の差異を表す)」

health considerations「健康面の配慮」

from countries where beer drinking is not common.

　　Communication modes have much to do with the decline of the pub as well. The Internet, digital entertainment, and communication devices such as phones keep people connected to a specific group of selected people. Such people find little interest in engaging in face-to-face communication with strangers or even people around them with whom they have little in common. Today, people seem to be more selective about socializing. They value privacy more strongly. Previously, people seemed to feel that they needed to try to get along with people with whom they shared a living area.

　　Government deregulation and regulation have also had a negative impact on the British pub. Breweries used to have a relationship with individual pubs, but that practice was stopped late in the 1980s. After that, large companies began to buy up many pubs. Rental fees for pubs then increased. Moreover, pubs are often sold when the parent company can make a profit on the land sale. Finally, anti-smoking laws launched by the government have also helped to keep customers away.

　　During World War I, pubs had to close down in the afternoons so that workers could focus on their jobs. This custom continued until the 1980s, when pubs began staying open all day. In 2003, they began closing later at night. At the time, it seemed as though these changes were helping to create a brighter future for pubs, but on the contrary, it now seems that this was the start of changes that will result in fewer and fewer of one of Britain's great cultural and historical institutions: the pub.

✳ COMPREHENSION

英文の内容に関する質問の答えとして適切なものをa～cから選びましょう。

1. During World War I, pubs in Britain started to:
    a. stay open all day. b. shut down later at night. c. close for part of the day.
2. Which is **not** a result of government involvement in the pub industry?
    a. Anti-smoking laws keep some pub visitors away.
    b. Large brewing companies no longer support pubs.
    c. A tax on beer has been going up since the 1980s.
3. Which is true about the decrease in the number of people going to pubs?
    a. Young people are not interested in getting to know people living nearby.
    b. More people smoke, so the number of customers at pubs has increased.
    c. Immigrants from other countries prefer cocktails to hard liquor and beer.
4. What was true of pubs in the past, according to the story?
    a. People did not go to pubs, as they liked drinking beer from supermarkets.
    b. The pub often served as a community social center for towns and villages.
    c. Until 1980, pubs stayed open all day to keep workers focused on their jobs.
5. According to the story, what is one danger facing pubs in the future?
    a. Tobacco companies will not support them because of anti-smoking laws.
    b. The British government will do everything in its power to save pubs.
    c. Pubs will decrease in number and possibly become extinct.

✳ SUMMARY

DL 009　CD1-32

次の（　）内に、与えられた文字で始まる適切な語を1語ずつ入れ、音声を聞いて確認しましょう。

　It seems that we will find ①(f　　　　) pubs in the future in Britain.　This important cultural and historic ②(i　　　　) may even disappear.

　One of the reasons for the ③(d　　　　) in the number of people going to pubs is the way people ④(c　　　　). It seems that young people are not very interested in getting to know people who live in the same ⑤(n　　　　).

　⑥(G　　　　) regulation and deregulation also affect pubs.　For example, large brewing companies no longer ⑦(s　　　　) pubs.　A pub will be sold if a ⑧(p　　　　) can be made.

　Drinking ⑨(h　　　　) and customs have changed, too.　For example, ⑩(i　　　　) to Britain from other countries do not often go to pubs.

DIALOGUE

次の会話の音声を聞いて、（　）内に1語ずついれましょう。

（TheoとRolindaは夕食後に新聞を読んでいます）

R: Oh, no, Theo! According to this newspaper article, there is going to be a ①(　　　) on horse and carriage rides in Central Park in New York City.

T: Wow! You have been looking forward to doing that next January when we go there.

R: It would be so romantic, riding around Central Park ②(　　　) ③(　　　) ④(　　　), listening to the clopping of the horse's feet.

T: Why is it going to stop? Were any reasons given?

R: It says here that the mayor finds this to be ⑤(　　　) to animals. So he wants to introduce electric, old-style classic cars to replace the horses and carriages.

T: I bet a lot of people are going to be unhappy with that situation.

R: You guessed correctly. 64% of the people living in New York ⑥(　　　) the horses and carriages.

T: In all fairness, Rolinda, it must be hard for the horses to stay in a big city like New York all the time.

R: But Theo, it says here that they get five weeks of vacation ⑦(　　　) ⑧(　　　) ⑨(　　　) each year. Also, they are not allowed to work on excessively hot or cold days.

T: Their working conditions are better than most humans'. I hope they are going to discuss the situation carefully before all of those horse caretakers ⑩(　　　) their jobs.

Notes▸ horse and carriage ride「馬車乗り」　clop「パカパカという音」　in all fairness「出来る限り公正であるためには」

✲ COMPREHENSION

上のDialogueの内容に関する質問の答えとして適切なものをa〜cから選びましょう。

1. When are Theo and Rolinda going to visit New York City?
   a. Next spring.　　**b.** Next autumn.　　**c.** Next winter.
2. Why does the mayor want to stop the horse and carriage rides?
   a. The drivers charge tourists too much money for rides.
   b. Cars cannot move easily with horses and carriages in the way.
   c. He believes that pulling a carriage is too hard on a horse.

Unit **3**　The Pub, an Endangered British Species　17

✳︎✳︎✳︎ VOCABULARY BUILDING

A 次の太字の語が同じ対比を表すように、空欄に入る適切な語をa～cから選びましょう。

1. **Brewery** is to **beer** as _____ is to **movie**.
   a. factory **b.** tannery **c.** studio
2. **Pub** is to **decline** as **cell phones** are to _____.
   a. regret **b.** increase **c.** costs
3. **Immigration** is to **population** as **reading** is to _____.
   a. knowledge **b.** library **c.** community
4. **Drink** is to **beverage** as **underground** is to _____.
   a. subway **b.** cloud **c.** bury
5. **Sale** is to **sail** as **feet** is to _____.
   a. hand **b.** body **c.** feat

B 接頭辞を持つ語が選択肢に含まれています。次の空欄にあてはまる適切な語をa～bから選びましょう。

1. Jerry, you cannot even consider going to the protest. It is _____. You will destroy your chances of getting a good job.
   a. thinkable **b.** unthinkable
2. Wow, that is a great price for that furniture set. I did not know this shop would have such _____ merchandise because it is so well-known.
   a. expensive **b.** inexpensive
3. Because of government _____, it is becoming harder and harder to open up a new business. There is just too much red tape.
   a. regulation **b.** deregulation
4. I heard that Thomas is going to _____ from Canada soon. His wife is from Tokyo, so they are going to settle down there.
   a. immigrate **b.** emigrate
5. You cannot drive home after having a beer at the bar, Al. That may be _____ in the U.S., but not here in Japan.
   a. legal **b.** illegal

Unit 4
Sleep Habits in the Mammal Kingdom

よく8時間の睡眠は必要だと言われます。7時間しか眠らないと活気を失うし、授業中や仕事中に眠たくなると言われます。睡眠は何時間取りますか。人間にも朝型、夜型の人などいろいろなタイプの人がいます。哺乳動物を見ても睡眠の取り方は千差万別です。あなたの睡眠の取り方はどんな哺乳動物と似ているでしょうか。

✲ VOCABULARY PREVIEW

次の空欄にあてはまる適切な語を a～c から選びましょう。

1. A mouse is an herbivore. It eats only plants while a tiger is a _____ animal. In other words, it hunts other animals in order to eat meat.
   a. predatory   **b.** peculiar   **c.** punctual
2. Diurnal animals sleep at night while _____ animals sleep during the day.
   a. numb   **b.** nimble   **c.** nocturnal
3. If you get sleepy in the afternoon, it is better to take a short _____ rather than drink coffee or tea.
   a. nap   **b.** neigh   **c.** nod
4. I flew from Canada to Japan last week, so I am still suffering from _____.
   a. diabetes   **b.** jet lag   **c.** insomnia
5. I like the _____ light, the time of day just before the sun comes up or just after it goes down, when there is only weak light.
   a. dawn   **b.** crepuscular   **c.** omnivorous

READING

How much sleep did you get last night? Because you are human, you were supposed to sleep about eight hours, which is considered healthy. However, most likely some of the students around you slept three hours, some slept ten, and others slept five. It is possible that some of your classmates took a nap during an economics lecture (not English, hopefully) to catch up on the sleep they missed during the night. Perhaps some just need more sleep than others. For sure, each student had a different reason for varying his or her sleeping time. The same happens with animals. The amount of sleep a mammal gets depends on many factors.

From time to time, you might find that you need a short nap. Animals are no different from us in this respect. Meat-eating mammals, or carnivores, such as dogs, cats, and lions, are famous for their long naps; nothing is going to hunt them. Rabbits, on the other hand, will hide when they take their very short naps. Mice do the same because they fear predators. For these creatures, alertness is just as important as sleep. Like a rabbit, you might take a short nap to avoid problems with a predatory professor. The teacher would not eat you if you slept during the lesson, but you might get scolded or punished.

If you had a night job, you might sleep during the day. This would make you nocturnal, and you would join many in the animal kingdom. This is one way in which nature balances food. Bats, for example, sleep all day. At night, they emerge when insects, their favorite food, are around. Some animals, such as the badger, have difficulty making seasonal adjustments. Much like a jet-lagged human, these animals cannot change their internal rhythms to match daylight. Therefore, during the summer, it is possible to see them walking about before

Notes

catch up on ~「~を取り戻す」

for sure「確かに」

mammal「哺乳動物」

in this respect「この点において」
carnivore「肉食動物」

predator「捕食動物」
alertness「用心深いこと」

badger「アナグマ」

darkness falls. Summer days are longer, but their sleeping time, about ten hours, does not change. In colder seasons, they move about only in darkness.

In addition to nocturnal mammals, which sleep during the day, and diurnal mammals, which sleep at night, there is another pattern common in mammals. Crepuscular mammals appear at twilight and dawn. Have you ever wondered why you often see deer just before nightfall? These shy animals like to come out when most of the others are gone. In desert regions, many creatures follow crepuscular patterns because it is the best time of the day to find water. Twilight and dawn are the times when many creatures move about the desert; suitable temperatures likely play a part in this as well.

Which of these types of animals do you most closely resemble? Do you enjoy staying awake at night like a fox or a raccoon? Do you sleep just two or three hours a night, like a giraffe, or eight hours, like a pig or a rabbit? Do you go to sleep on Friday night and wake up Monday morning, much like a bear hibernating? It is interesting to see how creatures rest, or sleep, to fit their lifestyles and habitats. One thing, however, is certain. Every mammal needs rest. This process is no less important, it seems, for humans, but unlike most mammals, we do not fit into one general pattern or category. It is sometimes said that the ability to think and reason distinguishes humans from other creatures. This is probably why sleep patterns vary so much for humans.

Notes

diurnal「昼行性の」
crepuscular「薄暮活動性の」

shy「臆病な」

raccoon「アライグマ」

hibernate「冬眠する」
habitat「生息地」
no less important「重要さは言うまでもない」

distinguish「区別する」

✳ COMPREHENSION

英文の内容に関する質問の答えとして適切なものをa〜cから選びましょう。

1. Which of the following statements applies to rabbits?
   a. Sleep is just as important as staying alert.
   b. Night is a good time for them to find insects.
   c. Long naps help them hunt more skillfully.
2. What is a nocturnal mammal going to do?
   a. Stay awake during the day.　　b. Sleep only before the sun rises.
   c. Stay awake during the night.
3. Which of the following mammals most likely sleeps the least, according to the story?
   a. A badger.　　　　b. A giraffe.　　　　c. A pig.
4. Hibernation means _____.
   a. spending a long amount of time sleeping
   b. sleeping for very short amounts of time
   c. living on plants and vegetables only
5. Why can a badger be seen during the summer months?
   a. It hibernates during the winter months.
   b. It sleeps for a fixed period of time all year.
   c. It has become crepuscular over time.

✳ SUMMARY

DL 012　　CD1-39

次の（　）内に、与えられた文字で始まる適切な語を1語ずついれ、音声を聞いて確認しましょう。

　Like other ①(m　　　) in the animal kingdom, the amount of time we sleep differs. This depends on many ②(f　　　).

　Meat-eating animals often take long ③(n　　　). They are able to sleep for long periods of time because no animals ④(h　　　) them. Other animals such as rabbits sleep for very short periods of time; they need to be ⑤(a　　　).

　⑥(N　　　) mammals sleep by day, while crepuscular animals, such as deer, come out just after the sun sets and then again before it ⑦(r　　　). Many mammals in the ⑧(d　　　) do this because it is a good time to find water.

　Unlike most mammal groups, humans have a ⑨(v　　　) of different sleep patterns. They have the ability to ⑩(t　　　) and reason.

DIALOGUE

次の会話の音声を聞いて、（　）内に1語ずつ入れましょう。

（Theo と Rolinda は夕食後に雑誌を読んでいます）

R: Theo, you always say that you could not ①(　　　) ②(　　　) ③(　　　) ④(　　　) sleep. Well… here is some good news! Many famous people also had trouble sleeping.

T: OK, Rolinda, go ahead and ⑤(　　　) ⑥(　　　) of me, just because you can fall asleep at the snap of your fingers. Anyway, who are these people?

R: Thomas Edison was one! He thought sleep was ⑦(　　　) ⑧(　　　) ⑨(　　　) time, so he took short naps only when he got tired. Wow… he thought bathing was a waste of time, too.

T: Maybe that is why he was an inventor and spent so much time alone.

R: Leonardo da Vinci used to get into bed early, but he had a ⑩(　　　) of re-thinking through his whole day.

T: Does that magazine mention anyone else?

R: Uh, huh. Winston Churchill. He spent a lot of time in bed, but he did not sleep much. It says that he kept two beds and ⑪(　　　) from one to another, trying to get sleepy.

T: Wow, those are all great people. Now I don't feel so bad about sleeping poorly.

R: Well, Mr. Genius, it is ⑫(　　　) midnight. I hope you are feeling tired.

Notes▶ at the snap of one's fingers 「指をはじいてパチンと鳴らすと」　sleep poorly 「よく寝られない」

✳ COMPREHENSION

上のDialogueの内容に関する質問の答えとして適切なものを a ～ c から選びましょう。

1. What does the magazine article imply about Leonardo da Vinci?
    a. He would look back over the events of his day.
    b. He would move from bed to bed to get sleepy.
    c. He would take drugs in order to fall asleep.

2. What did Theo suggest about Thomas Edison?
    a. People stayed away from him because he seldom took a bath.
    b. Experts found he was a genius because he took short naps.
    c. Though he spent a lot of time in bed, he slept very little.

Unit **4**　Sleep Habits in the Mammal Kingdom　　23

✳︎✳︎✳︎ VOCABULARY BUILDING

A 次の太字の語が同じ対比を表すように、空欄に入る適切な語をa～cから選びましょう。

1. **Herbivore** is to **plants** as **carnivore** is to _____.
   a. trees   b. meat   c. vegetables
2. **Nocturnal** is to **diurnal** as **dawn** is to _____.
   a. evening   b. sunrise   c. dusk
3. **Mammal** is to **fox** as _____ is to **crocodile**.
   a. amphibian   b. invertebrate c. reptile
4. **Hibernation** is to **bears** as _____ is to **birds**.
   a. insomnia   b. nap   c. migration
5. **Summer** is to **winter** as **scold** is to _____.
   a. adjust   b. praise   c. emerge

B それぞれ4語の中で1つだけ他の3語の範疇（カテゴリー）に入らないものがあります。例にならって、その1語と範疇を答えましょう。

例: Russia   Brazil   Canada   Japan
   CATEGORY: You could take out Japan and write *Large Countries* as the category.
   You could take out Brazil and write *Countries in the Northern Hemisphere*.

1. pig   turtle   deer   rabbit
   CATEGORY: _____

2. one   three   seven   ten
   CATEGORY: _____

3. Farsi   American   German   Japanese
   CATEGORY: _____

4. aikido   judo   bowling   kendo
   CATEGORY: _____

5. Edison   Benz   Churchill   Bell
   CATEGORY: _____

Unit 5 The Secret Behind the Image

"American Gothic" © The Art Institute of Chicago

この『アメリカン・ゴシック』という絵画を初めて見た人はいるかもしれませんが、非常に有名な絵なのです。1930年代、若きアメリカは世界に独自の文学、美術、そして演劇を誇示したがったのです。これらの分野ではヨーロッパに対して「劣等感」のようなものを感じていました。この絵はヨーロッパスタイルの技法要素を取り入れながらも、そこから何か新しいものを創り出そうと、アメリカのテーマを組み入れたものです。この絵が成功を収めた裏にはある秘密が隠されています。その秘密とは何か、またテーマとは何でしょう。

✻ VOCABULARY PREVIEW

次の空欄にあてはまる適切な語をa〜cから選びましょう。

1. I am going to visit the National Museum tomorrow. There is a very good _____ on 19th century American painters. Do you want to join me?
   a. auction **b.** continent **c.** exhibit

2. That drawing does not show anything or anybody real or realistic. It is just _____, a lot of strange lines and unusual patterns.
   a. practical **b.** fundamental **c.** abstract

3. That play was really funny, yet it taught us something important and critical about how the government actually works. It was a clever _____.
   a. satire **b.** fantasy **c.** tragedy

4. An illustration of a snowman often _____ winter. In other words, when we see it, we know right away which season that person is talking about.
   a. produces **b.** interprets **c.** symbolizes

5. The Yankees' star pitcher is going to retire at the end of the season, so they will have a _____ to him at the stadium before the game. The fans want to show their respect and admiration for him.
   a. tribute **b.** movement **c.** nostalgia

READING

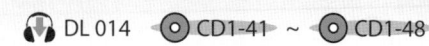

Grant Wood is considered to be a truly great "American" artist. Throughout his life, he drew and painted scenes from the "real America," the America of the western farm states. He helped create groups to support the careers of struggling artists. Also, he often provided his artistic talents to neighborhood businesses for small jobs. He would charge them based on their means to pay. He seemed to care a lot about ordinary people.

Though it is often hard to choose one painting by an artist that would be considered his or her classic, Grant Wood had one: American Gothic. A strong supporter of Regionalism, a movement in American painting that focused on local, realistic themes over abstract ones, this painting showed two ordinary, hard-working, farmers from the Iowa plains. It was typical among Grant's themes.

Painted in 1930, it was an instant success. Wood had it exhibited at the Art Institute of Chicago, where it won a $300 prize. Gertrude Stein, the famous writer and intellectual, called it a masterpiece, as did most art critics. However, many assumed that it was a satire of life in small towns in the countryside, showing narrow-minded, repressed people. This interpretation of the painting spread throughout the world.

Wood was furious. Not only did he reject this interpretation completely, but he explained his intention in creating the work: It was meant to show the hard-working American pioneer spirit that ordinary people all over the Midwest displayed. It was a tribute to the hard-working ordinary men and women of America's heartland.

In the painting, we see a stiff-looking man holding a pitchfork, which symbolizes hard work. Grant also revealed that the woman in the painting was supposed to be the man's unmarried daughter, yet many mistook her to be the man's wife. Wood put a nineteenth century apron on her to symbolize the values of early American pioneers. He applied skills that he had picked up from his travels on the European continent and studies of northern European art. For example, he produced a Gothic style house and a northern Renaissance atmosphere. It was strongly reminiscent of work done by the Dutch masters. Rarely had people in the Midwest, or the art world, for that matter, seen such a clever artistic combination of theme and technique.

This combination of American themes with European techniques was a great success. People were naturally eager to find the couple that Wood had used as a model for this famous painting. On this point, however, Grant remained silent.

The fact is that the couple really did not exist, at least not as they were presented in the painting. People had overlooked something else very important: Wood was an artist, and he had used one more element in this painting that is common to artists. He had used his imagination.

The man in the painting was his dentist, Dr. Byron McKeeby. The woman was his sister, Nan. To her dying days, she complained, "I don't know why so many people think I was the farmer's wife. I wish Grant had been more open about this!" According to another famous American artist, Norman Rockwell, the past is said to have been a time when we cared more about our family and neighbors. Grant Wood demonstrated this value in his most famous painting. He cared so much about his family and neighbors that he put the faces of two of them into his master work.

Notes

Gothic style house「ゴシック風の家」
Renaissance atmosphere「ルネッサンス（ほぼ14～17世紀の文芸復興期）的な雰囲気」
reminiscent「思い出させる」
the Dutch masters 1605年～1680年のオランダ黄金期に活躍したRembrandt, Vermeer, Frans Hals 等の画家たち
Rarely had people...seen ～ = People... had rarely seen ～の倒置形
for that matter「その点では」
were eager to ～「～したいと思った」

To her dying days「彼女が死ぬまで」

this 自分が農夫の妻と思われていたこと
Norman Rockwell「ノーマン・ロックウェル(1894～1978年)」(アメリカの画家、イラストレーター)
this value 家族や隣人を大事にしたこと

❋ COMPREHENSION

英文の内容に関する質問の答えとして適切なものをa～cから選びましょう。

1. Which of the following is true about Grant Wood?
   a. He often helped local people with projects and charged them little money.
   b. He was a loner who fought frequently with art dealers and other artists.
   c. He painted scenes from the European Renaissance using American techniques.
2. Who served as the male model in the famous painting "American Gothic"?
   a. A Dutch master.   b. Norman Rockwell.   c. A dentist.
3. Who did Nan, Wood's sister, portray in the painting?
   a. The farmer's wife.   b. The farmer's daughter.   c. The farmer's mother.
4. Which of the following in this painting was not influenced by Wood's study and travels in Europe?
   a. The building.   b. The atmosphere.   c. The signature.
5. What did the apron in the painting symbolize?
   a. Traditional values.   b. Hard work.   c. Poverty.

❋ SUMMARY

DL 015   CD1-49

次の（　）内に、与えられた文字で始まる適切な語を1語ずついれ、音声を聞いて確認しましょう。

　Grant Wood was one of the most ①(f　　　　) American artists of all time. His ②(m　　　　), or finest work, was "American Gothic," which he painted in 1930. Most artists considered it a great ③(s　　　　).

　The painting portrayed two people working on a ④(f　　　　), a man and his daughter, though most people mistook the woman as the man's ⑤(w　　　　). The painting was a tribute to Americans working hard in ⑥(a　　　　); the Midwest was the place where this profession was most common.

　The painting was praised highly for its original style. Wood ⑦(c　　　　) an American theme with European techniques. He picked up these techniques not only through his studies, but by ⑧(t　　　　) around Europe.

　People were surprised to find out how the painting was done. The models were not actually farmers, but Wood's ⑨(d　　　　) and his ⑩(s　　　　). Wood loved people; he used two very close to him in his most famous work of art.

DIALOGUE

DL 016　CD1-50

次の会話の音声を聞いて、（　）内に1語ずついれましょう。

（RolindaとTheoは夕食後に読書をしています）

R: Theo, have you ever seen this painting?
T: The "Mona Lisa"? Sure, everyone knows it. It is probably the most famous ①(　　　　) in the world.
R: She is smiling. I wonder why?
T: Who knows? Probably everyone smiled for a portrait painting.
R: It took da Vinci four years to paint this. Moreover, Francesco Giocondo, the rich merchant who ②(　　　) da Vinci, fired him.
T: Maybe he did not like the way da Vinci painted.
R: No, ③(　　　) ④(　　　) in this book that he just got tired of waiting. Da Vinci was always designing buildings and inventing things, such as flying machines.
T: I saw the Mona Lisa on my trip to France ⑤(　　　) ⑥(　　　) ⑦(　　　). I had no idea that da Vinci never finished it.
R: No, Theo, after Giocondo fired him, da Vinci did finish it quickly, took it to France, and sold it to the king for ⑧(　　) ⑨(　　　) ⑩(　　　) ⑪(　　　) money.
T: Wow, Rolinda! What a story! Say ... maybe she was smiling because she didn't have to ⑫(　　　) for this portrait any longer!

Notes▶ fire「解雇する」　did finish = finished より強調される

✳ COMPREHENSION

上のDialogueの内容に関する質問の答えとして適切なものをa～cから選びましょう。

1. According to Rolinda's book, why was da Vinci fired by Giocondo?
   a. He repainted the portrait of Lisa del Giocondo over and over again.
   b. He had secretly promised to sell the painting to the king of France.
   c. He took too much time to finish the portrait of Giocondo's wife.
2. Why does Theo think that Mona Lisa is smiling in the portrait?
   a. She is happy about her marriage to a rich merchant.
   b. She is happy that she does not have to be a model any more.
   c. She is happy that da Vinci will not be paid for his work.

Unit 5　The Secret Behind the Image　29

VOCABULARY BUILDING

A　次の太字の語が同じ対比を表すように、空欄に入る適切な語をa～cから選びましょう。

1. Grant Wood is to **painter** as **Haruki Murakami** is to _____.
   a. writer　　　　　　b. sculptor　　　　　　c. poet

2. The United States is to **country** as **Europe** is to _____.
   a. city　　　　　　　b. continent　　　　　　c. country

3. _____ is to **niece** as **brother** is to **sister**.
   a. Uncle　　　　　　b. Cousin　　　　　　　c. Nephew

4. Pitchfork is to **farmer** as _____ is to **painter**.
   a. rolling pin　　　　b. shovel　　　　　　　c. brush

5. Movie is to **theater** as **art exhibit** is to _____.
   a. university　　　　b. museum　　　　　　c. auction

B　次の空欄にあてはまる適切な語をa～cから選びましょう。

1. The red circle in the Japanese flag symbolizes the _____.
   a. moon　　　　　　b. pub　　　　　　　　c. sun

2. The Olympic torch symbolizes _____.
   a. sports unity　　　b. international brotherhood　　　c. the Olympic Games

3. A dove symbolizes _____.
   a. peace　　　　　　b. glue　　　　　　　　c. extinction

4. The Statue of Liberty symbolizes _____ for newcomers to the United States.
   a. taxes　　　　　　b. power　　　　　　　c. freedom

5. The colors of the French flag symbolize liberty, fraternity, and _____.
   a. equality　　　　　b. hope　　　　　　　　c. individuality

Unit 6 The Periodic Cicada, an Amazing Survivor

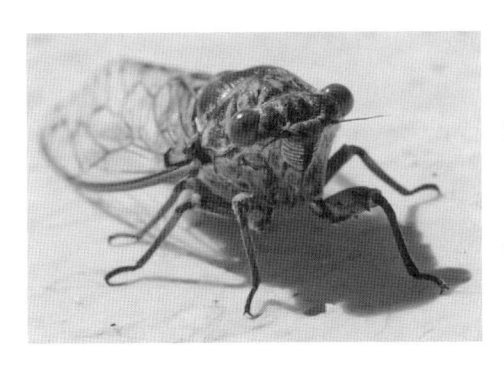

セミが地中から出てきて、寿命が尽きるまでは1週間とよく耳にしましたが、短命であることからそのようにいわれただけであって、実際は1ヶ月ほどは生きるようです。ただしセミが活躍する夏は暑く、また鳥などの天敵も多いため、1ヶ月の寿命を全うするものは少ないようです。アメリカにしか生息しないセミで毎世代正確に13年または17年で大量発生するセミがいます。この周期年数が素数であることから素数ゼミと呼ばれるセミです。さてここで問題です。この数字13と17の最小公倍数は？ またこの答えはこのセミとどのような関係があるのでしょうか。

✲ VOCABULARY PREVIEW

次の空欄にあてはまる適切な語を a～c から選びましょう。

1. My brother suffers from _____ headaches. He gets them, in other words, from time to time, though not very often.
   a. chronic **b.** periodic **c.** daily

2. The population is getting smaller in Japan because the rate of _____ is going down.
   a. reproduction **b.** death **c.** illness

3. We could not finish building our solar car. There were too many _____ involved with the project.
   a. successes **b.** predictions **c.** complexities

4. The new _____, which started in 2000, has been full of problems so far. I wonder if humankind will make it to the next one in 3000?
   a. decade **b.** year **c.** millennium

5. After we ran to the scene of the car accident, luckily, both drivers _____ from their cars without any injuries.
   a. emerged **b.** expected **c.** elevated

READING

In the world of nature, living things use many kinds of strategies to protect themselves from predators. Some animals, for example, are good at hiding. Others disguise themselves as objects or creatures that do not appeal to predators. Some just taste bad, or they give off powerful smells that keep predators away. Some grow thick shells to protect themselves. These are all common ways in which creatures try to survive in nature's food chain.

How has the periodic cicada survived so many millennia? Scientists believe there is a secret behind this insect's long presence on Earth: It has developed a highly unique reproductive cycle. Moreover, this approach seems to be based on principles of mathematics. While humans have used mathematics to create a highly technological and sophisticated world, these insects may thrive in nature thanks to math.

In southeastern parts of the United States, two types of periodic cicadas emerge from the ground every 13 years while 12 other types come out every 17 years. These cicadas are just a few centimeters long. They are slow and harmless. They are easy meals for birds, wasps, and other hungry creatures. However, when the cicadas come out of their eggs, they head underground, where they will spend 99% of their lives feeding off the roots of trees. Then, one summer, they will show up in huge numbers, 13 or 17 years later. As many as 40,000 cicadas may emerge in a single day. They then spend just a few weeks on this earth making lots of noise, hanging out in trees, and reproducing.

Birds and other creatures that might eat them are not ready for the sudden appearance of millions of cicadas. Some scientists think that if the cicadas came out every ten years, birds and other predators in the area might

Notes

disguise「変装する」

give off ~「~を発する」

food chain「食物連鎖」

millennia < millennium「1000年」の複数形

reproductive cycle「生殖周期」

sophisticated「高性能な」
thrive「成長する」

wasp「スズメバチ」

feed off ~「~から養分を得て育つ」

hang out ~「~に住む」

adjust to them. As the cicadas are easy prey, predators would come to expect the cicadas and depend on them as a food source. However, the 13 to 17 year cycle seems to protect them. Birds have regular sources of food, so the cicadas mean little to them.

13 and 17 are prime numbers. This is a number that cannot be divided by any other number, only one and itself. 12 and 18, for example, can both be divided by two, three, and six. Prime number appearances could be the reason that the periodic cicada is one of the longest living creatures in the insect world. If the cicadas were to come out every five and seven years, for example, the two types would meet every 35 years. This would lead to a mixing of the two groups. They might compete for food. Now, however, the two groups of cicadas can meet only once every 221 years. Because of this, there is no food shortage for the cicadas. Moreover, predators forget that millions of cicadas will come. Of course, some are eaten, but most survive.

Ever since humans first appeared on this planet, they have been trying to understand nature. Math has helped them in their search for answers to nature's many mysteries. It is a code that helps to solve riddles and understand complexities.

Prime numbers serve as the building blocks of mathematics. From mathematics, we get the basis for science. Two types of cicadas appear every 13 years; 12 of them appear every 17 years. Why not every 12, 15, or 16 years? Are cicadas using an important code that helps them to survive?

Notes

food source「食料の供給源」

prime number「素数（1とその数以外に約数がない正の整数）」

code「コード、記号」

building blocks「基礎資料単位」

✱ COMPREHENSION

英文の内容に関する質問の答えとして適切なものを a ～ c から選びましょう。

1. Which seems to be true about the survival strategy of periodic cicadas?
    a. They give off a powerful smell to keep predators away.
    b. They are covered by strong shells that are difficult to eat through.
    c. They come into the world only during certain numbered years.
2. Which is **not** true about the periodic cicadas?
    a. They come out in the southeastern part of the United States.
    b. Most of the broods of cicadas come out every 17 years.
    c. Most of them are eaten by birds and other predators.
3. Why is it helpful that the groups of cicadas meet so seldom?
    a. There should be enough food for all of them to eat.
    b. Birds expect them, so they can consume more of them.
    c. Math has helped to solve many of nature's mysteries.
4. Why are so few of the cicadas eaten after they come out?
    a. They are slow and harmless insects.
    b. Predators already have regular food sources.
    c. Other creatures enjoy the cicadas' singing.
5. How do periodic cicadas spend most of their lives?
    a. Making noise.   b. Feeding on tree roots.   c. Chasing other insects.

✱ SUMMARY

🎧 DL 018   💿 CD1-58

次の（　）内に、与えられた文字で始まる適切な語を1語ずつ入れ、音声を聞いて確認しましょう。

　　Have scientists discovered the ①(s　　　　) for the long survival rate of the periodic cicadas? The answer may lie in the mysteries of ②(m　　　　).

　　By appearing just every 13 or 17 years, the groups of ③(i　　　　) do not meet very often. Therefore, the different types do not ④(m　　　　), or come together, easily. Also, they do not have to ⑤(c　　　　) for sources of food.

　　Moreover, periodic cicadas spend most of their lives ⑥(u　　　　), feeding off the roots of trees. After they come out, they spend their short lives above ground making ⑦(n　　　　) and ⑧(r　　　　).

　　Perhaps math will help the periodic cicada to avoid ⑨(e　　　　). In other words, these cicadas will probably exist in ⑩(n　　　　) for a long time.

DIALOGUE

DL 019 CD1-59

次の会話の音声を聞いて、（　）内に1語ずついれましょう。

(Theo と Rolinda は夕食後に読書をしています)

T: Rolinda, quick, get a can of ①(　　　　　). There is a bee in here!

R: Theo, don't you dare kill that bee! Along with ants, bees are the most amazing of nature's creatures.

T: What am I going to do if it ②(　　　　) me?

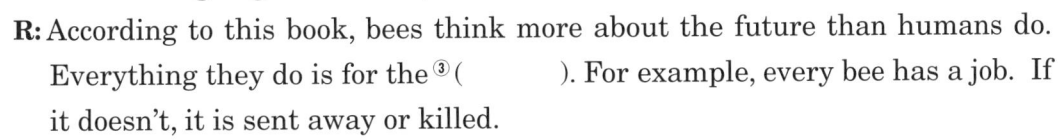

R: According to this book, bees think more about the future than humans do. Everything they do is for the ③(　　　　). For example, every bee has a job. If it doesn't, it is sent away or killed.

T: Boy, I am glad that my brothers aren't bees.

R: They choose one flower each day from which to take pollen to make ④(　　　　). Also, nothing foreign can come into the hive. If there is the slightest problem, the queen will order all of the bees to leave the hive and construct a new one.

T: Don't they leave when there's smoke? I mean, they are ⑤(　　　　) ⑥(　　　　) smoke, right?

R: They are not afraid. They just become calm. This book says that they are ⑦(　　　　) their energy. In case a fire comes that will destroy the hive, they have to be ready to do a lot of work.

T: Wow... say, Rolinda, let me read that. And quick, open a window!

Notes▶ don't you dare kill「殺さないで」　hive = beehive「ハチの巣」　pollen「花粉」

✲ COMPREHENSION

上のDialogueの内容に関する質問の答えとして適切なものをa〜cから選びましょう。

1. What does Theo imply about his brothers?
   a. They are likely to cause trouble as bees do.
   b. They do not like to work very hard.
   c. They consume lots of sweets.

2. Which of the following is true about bees?
   a. When the time is right, the king will order the hive to be moved.
   b. A bee will take pollen from just one type of flower each day.
   c. Bees cannot breathe when they encounter smoke.

Unit **6** The Periodic Cicada, an Amazing Survivor

VOCABULARY BUILDING

A 次の太字の語が同じ対比を表すように、空欄に入る適切な語をa～cから選びましょう。

1. **Periodic** is to **constant** as **sometimes** is to _____.
   a. never　　　　　　　b. occasionally　　　　c. always
2. **Cicada** is to **insect** as _____ is to **amphibian**.
   a. frog　　　　　　　　b. crow　　　　　　　　c. gorilla
3. **Come out** is to **emerge** as **buy** is to _____.
   a. sell　　　　　　　　b. purchase　　　　　　c. low
4. **Predator** is to **prey** as **police officer** is to _____.
   a. pray　　　　　　　　b. law　　　　　　　　　c. criminal
5. **Harmless** is to **harmful** as **cheap** is to _____.
   a. broken　　　　　　　b. poor　　　　　　　　c. expensive

B 次の下線の語とほぼ同じ意味を表す語(句)をa～cから選びましょう。

1. For the past two centuries, humans have tried hard to develop a sophisticated world.
   a. just　　　　　　　　b. reasonable　　　　　c. advanced
2. Since my brother got a new job in New York, he has been thriving.
   a. struggling　　　　　b. succeeding　　　　　c. dating
3. Nuts are a great source of nutrition for winter animals.
   a. supply　　　　　　　b. exit　　　　　　　　c. location
4. The reproduction rate in developing countries is going down.
   a. growing food　　　　b. making babies　　　　c. saving money
5. There is a shortage of talent in this year's theater group.
   a. not enough　　　　　b. low height　　　　　c. large amount

Unit 7
The Story Behind a Modern Wonder Drug

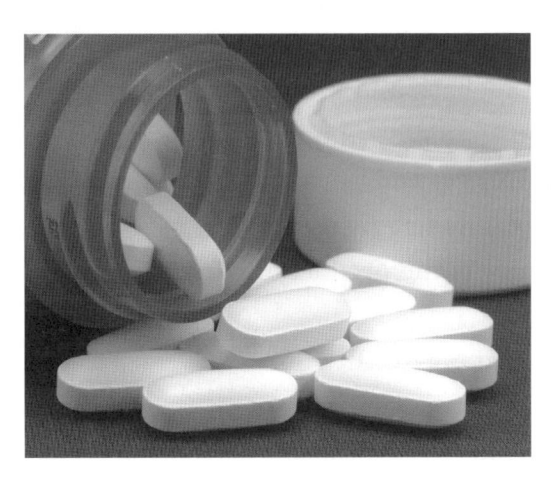

アスピリンを飲んだことがありますか。1800年代後半に出てきたこの薬は何百万という人々を救い、人々の痛みを和らげてきました。過去20年の間にアスピリンの新たなる使い道が発見されたりもしました。2014年に出された報告書では、この薬は乳がんの危険性を減らし、治すかもしれないというのです。この驚くべき薬の誕生について読んでみましょう。

✼ VOCABULARY PREVIEW

次の空欄にあてはまる適切な語を a ～ c から選びましょう。

1. Much of my family works in the _____ industry. My brothers own drugstores and my father still works in a factory where medicine is produced.
   a. aviation **b.** technological **c.** pharmaceutical

2. My uncle is the head of a small Protestant church. Unlike priests, however, _____ are church workers who can marry and have families.
   a. reverends **b.** nuns **c.** accountants

3. Cork trees do not have to be cut down in order to make corks for wine. Workers simply remove the outside layer of the tree, or the _____, which grows back in about nine years' time.
   a. branch **b.** roots **c.** bark

4. My professor just had his fourth book _____ by a large company. I hope that many people will buy and read it. It took him several years to write.
   a. written **b.** published **c.** invented

5. My mother's business has _____ from a small shop where she and her mother mended old clothing to a factory that employs 200 people.
   a. reduced **b.** evolved **c.** discovered

READING

The last time you had a headache or a fever, what did you do? Did you take aspirin? Many people keep a bottle at home. Many carry a container with them. However, aspirin does not only relieve headaches and reduce
5 pain. Scientists keep finding new uses for it. Aspirin can prevent heart attacks, strokes, cancer, and perhaps even Alzheimer's disease. Amazingly, this drug was not invented or discovered by one person; it is the product of a complex history.

10 The story of aspirin began in ancient Egypt. In 1862, Edwin Smith bought some old documents written on papyrus. The Rosetta Stone had been discovered not long before that, and Smith had studied hieratic, the language used by the Ancient Egyptians. Smith found
15 that his two long scrolls were about medicine. Part of the documents focused on pharmaceutical products used at that time. Though most of the plants were unknown, one was clear: Willow. Egyptians had used it as a pain killer. Later, historians found that Sumerians had used
20 willow as well.

The ancient Egyptians were extremely advanced in medicine. Medical treatment, however, seemed to regress over the following millennia. By the 1700s, that started to change. Around that time, in a town called
25 Chipping Norton in England, a reverend made an astonishing discovery, or re-discovery.

Edward Stone was sitting along the banks of the town river, which was lined with willow trees. He picked up a piece of willow bark by chance and placed it in his
30 mouth. He noticed a strange, bitter flavor. To him, it tasted like medicine he had once been given for an illness.

Stone gathered up some willow bark and decided to dry it completely. He then began giving it to people in

Notes

heart attack「心臓発作」
stroke「脳卒中」

papyrus「パピルス紙（古代エジプト・ギリシャ・ローマ時代の紙）」
hieratic「神官文字（象形文字を崩した筆記体文字）」
scroll「巻物」

Sumerian「シュメール人」

regress「後戻りする」

Chipping Norton「チッピング・ノートン（イギリスOxfordから北西29キロにある町）」

the town for various illnesses. Since there was no doctor in Chipping Norton at that time, many sick people came to Stone, as he was a man of religion. The reverend watched his patients carefully. He was convinced, after five years, that he had found something important.

Stone wrote to the president of the Royal Society. This was a famous organization of scientists and scholars that had been founded by the king in 1663. It published a journal called *Philosophical Transactions*, which introduced groundbreaking work in physics, astronomy, mathematics, natural philosophy, and more. Chances of having an article published by the society were extremely low, but Stone was lucky again. He happened to know the society's president. Moreover, his theory on willow bark was of interest to the scientifically-minded in the society. Stone's article was accepted.

By the end of the 1800s, many companies were making pain relievers. A scientist at the Bayer Company, however, stumbled upon aspirin when he found a key ingredient accidentally: An order was mixed up and he added a dye to his pain reliever. By chance, it was just what was needed to make aspirin.

In 1918, aspirin saved many lives in the Spanish Flu epidemic. By the 1950s, however, new pain relievers appeared, and people began to think of aspirin as old-fashioned. Around 2000, though, aspirin had made a miraculous comeback. Researchers found that aspirin helped blood to move more smoothly. In the following decade, scientists discovered that aspirin helped to prevent heart attacks and strokes.

Both medically and in the world of business, aspirin has proved itself, in various forms, a wonder drug over a span of several thousand years. Moreover, this inexpensive, easily obtained drug never seems to stop evolving.

Notes

Royal Society (of London)「（ロンドン）王立協会」

groundbreaking「草分けの、革新的な」
natural philosophy「自然哲学、物理学」

pain reliever「鎮痛剤」
Bayer Company「バイエル社」
stumble upon~「～に出くわす」

dye「色素」

Spanish Flu「スペイン風邪（A型ウイルスが原因の感冒）」

Unit **7** The Story Behind a Modern Wonder Drug

✼ COMPREHENSION

英文の内容に関する質問の答えとして適切なものをa～cから選びましょう。

1. In the last paragraph, what does the writer imply?
   a. That aspirin costs little and can be bought easily.
   b. That aspirin is out of date, but marketed cleverly.
   c. That aspirin prevents better drugs from being developed.
2. Which is a key ingredient from nature in relieving pain?
   a. Willow.   b. Papyrus.   c. Dye.
3. What happened to aspirin in the middle of the twentieth century?
   a. Sales increased greatly because of the Spanish flu epidemic.
   b. Doctors discovered many new uses for aspirin, so sales increased.
   c. Sales decreased as new pain relievers took away aspirin's customers.
4. What helped Reverend Stone to get his article on willow bark published?
   a. There was a shortage of good material that year in the Royal Society journal.
   b. Stone's ability to read papyrus scrolls impressed the Royal Society committee.
   c. The head of the Royal Society at that time was an acquaintance of Stone's.
5. When the papyrus scrolls had been translated, what did scholars find?
   a. Reverend Stone had made up information in his article on willow bark.
   b. High-quality medical treatment was available thousands of years ago.
   c. Edwin Smith had discovered the secret purpose of the Rosetta Stone.

✼ SUMMARY

🎧 DL 021   💿 CD1-69

次の（　）内に、与えられた文字で始まる適切な語を1語ずつ入れ、音声を聞いて確認しましょう。

　Aspirin was not ①(d　　　　) by one person. It evolved over thousands of years. The ancient Egyptians and Sumerians used willow, which is a key ②(i　　　　) in aspirin, to relieve ③(p　　　) for those suffering from medical problems.

　Most of the credit for aspirin goes to Edward Stone, a ④(r　　　　) who worked in a small town in England. One day, while he was sitting on a river ⑤(b　　　), he happened to put a piece of willow ⑥(b　　　) in his mouth. He noticed that it tasted like ⑦(m　　　　) he had once been given for an illness. Stone then studied willow's effects on his ⑧(p　　　　). Soon after, he wrote a paper on his findings, which was ⑨(p　　　　) in an important journal.

　Today, aspirin is used for such problems as heart attacks and ⑩(s　　　　).

DIALOGUE

DL 022　CD1-70

次の会話の音声を聞いて、（ ）内に1語ずついれましょう。

（Theo と Rolinda は夕食後に読書をしています）

R: Here is an interesting story. In 1602, a Spanish ship was sailing up the coast of California. ①(　　　　) ②(　　　　) ③(　　　　) of the crew was sick.

T: What was wrong with them?

R: Purple spots covered their bodies. The ④(　　　　) in their mouths swelled badly.

T: So they couldn't eat?

R: Right! Then these feverish men began dying, one by one. Suddenly, one of the seamen, who was less sick than the others, picked up a cactus fruit when they went ashore.

T: Let me guess … he ate it and he got better!

R: Yes! All of the crew members started eating them and they recovered from the sickness. It took many years to figure out that certain fruits and vegetables could ⑤(　　　　) this disease.

T: Isn't it amazing how humans make discoveries like that? That disease was scurvy, right?

R: Uh, huh. But here is the most interesting part … it wasn't until ⑥(　　　　) that a Hungarian scientist deduced that vitamin C was the key ⑦(　　　　).

T: That sounds a lot like the story of aspirin to me.

Notes▶ gums「歯茎」 feverish「熱のある」 figure out「理解する」 scurvy「壊血病」（ビタミンCの欠乏によって起こる病気。出血しやすくなり、歩行困難などの症状が現れる）」 deduce「推論する」

✳ COMPREHENSION

上の Dialogue の内容に関する質問の答えとして適切なものを a ～ c から選びましょう。

1. Where did the sailors in this story come from?
   a. Hungary.　　　**b.** The United States.　　　**c.** Spain.
2. What was the cure for scurvy?
   a. Vitamin C.　　　**b.** Aspirin.　　　**c.** Gum.

Unit **7** The Story Behind a Modern Wonder Drug

✳︎ VOCABULARY BUILDING

A 次の太字の語が同じ対比を表すように、空欄に入る適切な語をa〜cから選びましょう。

1. **Doctor** is to **hospital** as _____ is to **church**.
   a. inventor　　　b. butcher　　　c. reverend
2. **Willow** is to _____ as **cicada** is to **insect**.
   a. mammal　　　b. flower　　　c. tree
3. **Scroll** is to _____ as **crane** is to **bird**.
   a. medicine　　　b. beverage　　　c. paper
4. _____ is to **river** as **sidewalk** is to **road**.
   a. Source　　　b. Bank　　　c. Water
5. _____ is to **die** as **mourning** is to **morning**.
   a. Live　　　b. Funeral　　　c. Dye

B 同音異義語の選択肢が並んでいます。次の空欄にあてはまる適切な語をa〜bから選びなさい。

1. I cannot take this medicine out of _____. I take only natural herbs if I feel that I am ill.
   a. principal　　　b. principle
2. I have to return this book to the library at once. It is _____ by more than two months.
   a. overdo　　　b. overdue
3. The window broke during the storm. Now we're going to have to get a new _____ to replace the one that shattered.
   a. pain　　　b. pane
4. Which road do we take to get to the pharmacy? I checked the _____ on the Internet before leaving, but I seem to have taken a wrong turn.
   a. route　　　b. root
5. It is raining hard, so I will stay indoors and get some exercise on the _____ bicycle in my basement.
   a. stationary　　　b. stationery

Unit 8　Black Friday

　　Black Tuesday とは 1929 年から続いた世界経済の大不況の始まりを表す言葉で歴史の本にも載っています。Black Friday という言葉を耳にしたことがありますか。この言葉はアメリカでは Thanksgiving Day のあとの特別な買い物の日を表します。どこからこの言葉は生まれたのでしょうか。なぜその金曜日は黒と呼ばれるのでしょうか。この質問に対する答えがすぐに出てこなくても、全く心配する必要はありません。本文を読んでいけば、すぐに答えがわかりますから。

✲ VOCABULARY PREVIEW

次の空欄にあてはまる適切な語を a～c から選びましょう。

1. Some animals see the world in black, white, and shades of gray. They are _____.
   a. monotone　　　　**b.** near-sighted　　　　**c.** colorblind

2. Last year, my brother spent more money than he earned. He used his bank savings, but if he does not stop doing that next year, he will go into _____.
   a. profit　　　　**b.** debt　　　　**c.** lottery

3. Some say the world economy suffered a recession in 2008, but in my opinion, it was a(n) _____. So many people lost their jobs and had to live off their family savings.
   a. depression　　　　**b.** expression　　　　**c.** repression

4. I thought that records were _____, but my music teacher still buys them. He says that some types of music sound better on them than they do on CDs.
   a. obsolete　　　　**b.** inexpensive　　　　**c.** popular

5. Though the _____ for many large companies increased last year, more workers lost their jobs. This doesn't make sense to me.
   a. losses　　　　**b.** earnings　　　　**c.** accounting

READING

What is the busiest and most profitable shopping day of the year in the United States? Many people believe it is the day before Christmas. Many years ago, they would have been correct, but in recent years, the day after Thanksgiving has become the biggest shopping day of the year. Because Thanksgiving always falls on a Thursday, this big buying day has been given a nickname: Black Friday.

Most people have the wrong idea about where the name came from. One popular notion is connected with money. If a store does not sell enough or make a profit, we might say it is "in the red." When it is making money, we say it is "in the black." (American money is green in color; idioms are sometimes colorblind.) Actually, these expressions come from accounting, where debts are marked in red ink and earnings in black. Therefore, this misunderstanding makes sense. Many stores do operate in the red all year until Black Friday comes. The Christmas season then pushes them into "the black."

By the 1990s, Black Friday had become more popular than ever. Many people began heading to department stores and malls at 4:00 a.m. to take advantage of sale prices. By 2000, stores started opening even earlier. In 2013, in New York City, for example, Macy's, a large department store, opened at 8:00… in the evening, on Thanksgiving!

How did shoppers react? On that Black Friday, 15,000 people were waiting in line when the store opened its doors. More and more stores have decided to open on Thanksgiving; in 2012, sales totaled $810,000,000 on Thanksgiving. Is this a large amount? The following day, $11,200,000,000 was spent… in one day, on Black Friday.

The term "Black Friday" comes from Philadelphia.

The police department was responsible for creating the phrase in the 1950s. As more people came out to shop the day after Thanksgiving, which is a holiday for most, and more and more cars crowded the streets, the police worried about problems this increased activity would bring. Some people believe the police based "Black Friday" on another expression, "Black Tuesday." This was the day that the American stock market collapsed and the economy went into a long depression in 1929. This was indeed a dark day, but Black Friday is not black in this sense of the meaning.

Why do so many people decide to shop on a day when stores, streets, and parking lots are crowded? For one thing, sale prices are attractive. Large department stores often discount their goods by 50% on Black Friday. Many stores, however, are starting to do this on Thanksgiving. For tradition-minded Americans, this is problematic. Thanksgiving was once a day for rest, family, and happiness at home.

The future of Black Friday is uncertain. E-shopping may keep people away from malls and department stores. In 2012, 19.7% more people shopped on the Internet on Thanksgiving than ever in the past, while Black Friday e-shoppers rose by 9%. A poor economy in general may also affect Black Friday numbers in future years. Thanksgiving may take the place of Black Friday, making it obsolete as a special day.

Thanksgiving used to be a holiday to relax with the family. It seems that it has already become a day to race to the shopping malls for many. Will Black Friday survive societal and technological changes? Economics is a human science. One can only wait and see how people will behave as conditions change.

Notes

stock market「株式市場」
collapse「暴落する」

problematic「問題のある」

take the place of ~ = replace「~に取って代わる」

societal「社会の」

wait and see~「~を待って成り行きを見る」

☆ COMPREHENSION

英文の内容に関する質問の答えとして適切なものを a ～ c から選びましょう。

1. Which is now the busiest shopping day of the year in the United States?
   a. Black Tuesday.
   b. The day after Thanksgiving.
   c. The day before Christmas.
2. Which of the following is not a threat to shops concerning Black Friday?
   a. More people are shopping on the Internet.
   b. People are no longer interested in discounts.
   c. The economy in general may get worse.
3. Where does the term "Black Friday" come from?
   a. Stores become profitable on that day thanks to heavy shopping activity.
   b. Police were worried about problems arising from increased shopping.
   c. It is the anniversary of the start of the Great Depression of 1929.
4. What are tradition-minded Americans worried about, according to the story?
   a. Thanksgiving will no longer be a holiday for the family.
   b. Too many people will start shopping on the Internet.
   c. Discounts will become smaller at department stores.
5. What happened on Black Tuesday?
   a. Department stores made the most profit of all time on that day.
   b. Native Americans protested Thanksgiving as a crime against them.
   c. The world economy began a long and severe economic depression.

☆ SUMMARY

DL 024　CD2-09

次の（　）内に、与えられた文字で始まる適切な語を１語ずつ入れ、音声を聞いて確認しましょう。

　In the United States, the busiest and most ①(p　　　) shopping day of the year is ②(B　　) Friday. This is the day after ③(T　　　).

　People believe, incorrectly, that the term comes from ④(a　　　). They think that Black Friday pushes many stores' ⑤(p　　　) high, so they are no longer in the ⑥(r　　　), so to speak. The term was ⑦(c　　　) by the Philadelphia police department in the 1950s. Because so many ⑧(s　　　) came out on that day, the police worried that there would be lots of ⑨(p　　　).

　Some Americans worry that Black Friday is destroying Thanksgiving. This day is supposed to be a day of rest at home for ⑩(f　　　).

DIALOGUE

🔽 DL 025 ⏺ CD2-10

次の会話の音声を聞いて、（　）内に1語ずついれましょう。

(Theo と Rolinda は夕食後に新聞を読んでいます)

R: I can't believe what I am reading in this newspaper. There was so much ①(　　　) on Black Friday.

T: I guess that is why it is called Black Friday.

R: In Virginia, two men fought over a ②(　　　) ③(　　　). One man stabbed the other with a knife and then threatened him with a rifle.

T: That is crazy! How did the ④(　　　) ⑤(　　　) react?

R: It says here that they all ran back to the shopping center. Here is another ⑥(　　　) ⑦(　　　) from New Jersey. Two men had a fight over a television set.

T: Where were they?

R: In a department store. The manager came, then a police officer. One of the men would not ⑧(　　　), so the police officer used pepper spray to overpower and arrest him.

T: Well, if there were just two situations, I guess it's OK. Black Friday is a ⑨(　　　) day to be out shopping.

R: Theo, I read just two. There are many more stories. Do you want to hear more?

T: Uh… no thanks.

Notes▶ parking space 「駐車するスペース」　overpower 「取り押さえる」

✳ COMPREHENSION

上のDialogueの内容に関する質問の答えとして適切なものをa～cから選びましょう。

1. What were the two men in New Jersey fighting about?
   a. A can of pepper spray.　　b. A knife.　　c. A television.
2. What happened to one of the men who had a fight in Virginia?
   a. He was shot with a rifle.　　b. He was injured with a knife.
   c. He hid in the mall.

Unit **8** Black Friday　47

✸✸ VOCABULARY BUILDING

A 次の太字の語が同じ対比を表すように、空欄に入る適切な語を a ～ c から選びましょう。

1. **Thanksgiving** is to **November** as _____ is to **December**.
   a. Black Friday   b. Independence Day   c. Christmas
2. **Profit** is to **store** as _____ is to **university**.
   a. earning   b. knowledge   c. recession
3. **Depression** is to **economy** as _____ is to **weight**.
   a. loss   b. gain   c. stability
4. **Black** is to **red** as **expand** is to _____.
   a. stock   b. increase   c. contract
5. **Accounting** is to **money** as _____ is to **medicine**.
   a. pharmacology   b. economics   c. literature

B 空欄にあてはまる適切な色を表す語を選びましょう。ただし語は1度しか使えません。

1. My aunt is so good at gardening. She really has a _____ thumb.
2. Not only is it Monday, but it is raining hard. I am so _____.
3. That house is not haunted. Don't be _____; just go inside!
4. Tom gave our teacher another present yesterday. He is such a _____ nose!
5. When my mother saw my poor report card from school, she turned _____.
6. I want to start my own business, but it is so complicated. I am tired of all the _____ tape with the local government.

black	yellow	red
purple	green	blue
brown	white	orange

Unit 9 Getting High on Gardening

香港といえば、何が思い浮かびますか。近代的高層ビルが建ち並ぶ光景でしょうか。それとも夜景の有名な都市でしょうか。立派な天然の港でしょうか。有機野菜を栽培する農地でしょうか。

最初の3つにはうなずかれるのではないでしょうか。しかし、最後の答えには首をかしげるかもしれませんね。

香港にはほとんど未開発の土地がないので、当然疑問を持たれる人は多いと思います。しかしほとんど空いている土地がない都会にも、何とか農地を作ろうとしている人たちがいるのです。さてどのような工夫をして農地を作っているのでしょうか。

✲ VOCABULARY PREVIEW

次の空欄にあてはまる適切な語をa～cから選びましょう。

1. That farm does not use chemicals on its fruits and vegetables. It is _____.
   a. elite **b.** organic **c.** artificial
2. The _____ in California is very rich. Any kind of vegetable can grow there.
   a. soil **b.** air **c.** liquid
3. That bag is neither made of leather nor is it a designer brand, though it has a designer label on it. It is a fake, an _____.
   a. artifact **b.** imitation **c.** obstacle
4. If you use herbicides, you will kill unwanted plants. If you use pesticides, you will kill unwanted _____.
   a. crops **b.** prices **c.** insects
5. I don't like buying _____ from a gourmet food shop. It is too expensive, so I just buy ordinary fruit and vegetables at a supermarket.
   a. chemicals **b.** produce **c.** sand

READING

Kimbo Chan, 42, talks about why he suddenly quit his job as an investment banker and became a farmer. "Formaldehyde is sometimes sprayed on cabbage. There is melamine in the milk. Imitation soy sauce is made from hair clippings. I have heard that industrial chemicals are used on crops, too, chemicals that are not supposed to be used for agricultural purposes. We have to be careful about buying products from abroad."

Chan farms in a very unusual place: 18 stories up, on the rooftop of his apartment building. According to government sources in Hong Kong, there are approximately 100 such farms. Seven years ago, there were none. What led to this growth?

"It is logical," explains Osbert Lam, the owner of City Farm. "There is not enough land in Hong Kong to farm any longer, so the only place to go is up!"

High-priced organic food stores are opening all over Hong Kong, as they are in large cities all over the world. "This is not good," explains Jonathan Wang, a professor of biology. "I get the feeling sometimes that organic foods are a form of premium branding, not science. It is better quality food for people with more money."

With seven million people, Hong Kong has little farmland. It must import 90 percent of its produce in a territory that is crazy about vegetables. Moreover, 92% of that food comes from China. There are farms in the New Territories, but developers want to get that land from the nearly dead agricultural sector.

Professor Wang says that developers' money is not the only factor killing farming in Hong Kong. "There are typhoons. There is high humidity. The summers are unbearably hot. And finally, there is the soil. Our land is uncooperative."

Mr. Lam agrees with this, but he says there are alternatives. "We need to find the right mix when we grow something. Last year, for example, I imported soil from Europe. I had to sift, mix, and adjust my soil until I could grow certain things. When I grow potatoes, for instance, I need to add more sand to the mixture. If I grow strawberries, I need to add peat moss. One problem I have in farming, however, is the government. There is so much red tape in starting a rooftop farm here. This almost drove me away from farming."

Mr. Lam's farm, 14 stories above the busy streets of Hong Kong, offers many kinds of crops: turnips, pumpkins, carrots, potatoes, spinach, watermelons, chili peppers, and eggplant. He grows leafy vegetables in shallow boxes, and uses deeper boxes for vegetables with deep roots. Most of his gardening supplies come from Taiwan. "I am not rolling in money," Lam confesses, "but I love this work."

Professor Wang replies, "The world population is growing. We need to work on GM crops, not organic vegetables for rich people. Farmers must embrace science. Organic farming is a little like organized religion, or a cult. We need to raise crop outputs with herbicides, pesticides, and insecticides. People criticize agriculture in China, but the farmers there grow a lot. The prices are reasonable, too. With organic farming, we are missing the forest for the tree."

An elderly shopper said this: "Those organic vegetables look great, but look at this squash I bought at an ordinary market. It was grown in China. It is really cheap, and for an old woman like me, that is the only thing that matters. I cannot be worried about chemicals."

☸ COMPREHENSION

英文の内容に関する質問の答えとして適切なものをa～cから選びましょう。

1. Why are farms in Hong Kong being developed on the top of buildings?
   a. Farmers there like their land to be closer to the sun.
   b. High altitude means stronger breezes and better air.
   c. There is almost no undeveloped land in Hong Kong.
2. Which is an attractive point about organic vegetables?
   a. They are costly to grow.   b. They are free of chemicals.
   c. They require special soil.
3. Which of the following best summarizes Professor Wang's position?
   a. Farmers need to grow crops in great quantity; quality is not as important.
   b. It is unnecessary to worry about chemicals; they are not that bad for humans.
   c. The bureaucracy in Hong Kong is stopping creative farming from taking place.
4. In the story, a woman bought squash at an ordinary supermarket. Why?
   a. She is devoted to her usual fruit and vegetable seller.
   b. The price of the organically grown squash was high for her.
   c. Avoiding chemicals is important to the elderly in Hong Kong.
5. Which is **not** true about Mr. Lam's farming practices?
   a. He uses different sized containers for growing his vegetables.
   b. He mixes soil differently depending on the fruit or vegetable.
   c. He sometimes sprays chemicals on his vegetables to protect them.

☸ SUMMARY

DL 027　CD2-21

次の（　）内に、与えられた文字で始まる適切な語を1語ずついれ、音声を聞いて確認しましょう。

　　Hong Kong has little land for ①(a　　　　), so ②(o　　　　) farming now takes place on the ③(r　　　　) of high buildings.

　　There are many ④(o　　　　) to farming in Hong Kong. There are typhoons, the weather is very hot, and most of all, the ⑤(s　　　) is difficult to farm.

　　One professor believes that organic farming provides food only for ⑥(w　　　) people. Farmers should think about growing vegetables in greater ⑦(q　　　). To do so, herbicides and ⑧(i　　　　) are important.

　　For many, organic vegetables grown in Hong Kong are just too ⑨(e　　　　). However, they have become popular in large ⑩(c　　　) all over the world.

DIALOGUE

DL 028　CD2-22

次の会話の音声を聞いて、（　）内に1語ずついれましょう。

（Theo と Rolinda は夕食後に読書をしています）

T: Rolinda, I am really worried about the ①(　　　　) ②(　　　　　　). It is getting so large. How will humankind produce enough food?

R: I am reading about quinoa now. This might help. It provides calcium, iron, fiber, vitamin E, and it is a complete ③(　　　　　).

T: First, I have never heard of it, and second, can a lot of it be grown?

R: It can grow in poor, ④(　　　　) ⑤(　　　　　). It can put up with cold and droughts. Most scientists think it can be adapted to other places, but… it is protected.

T: What? The world needs something like this now.

R: It grows in ⑥(　　　) ⑦(　　　　). This is where potatoes came from originally. They adapted all over the world.

T: Scientists have to start working on this right away.

R: The seeds are ⑧(　　　　　) very carefully by the government there. It believes that quinoa belongs to the people of Bolivia.

T: Any food, any seeds should not belong to a government or ⑨(　　　　　). They should belong to people everywhere. Especially now.

Notes▶ quinoa「キノア（南米アンデス山脈産のアカザ科アカザ属の植物。葉をほうれん草と同様に食用にする）」 put up with ~「耐え忍ぶ」 the Andes「アンデス山脈（コロンビア及びベネズエラから Cape Horn まで南米西部を縦走する大山脈）」 Bolivia「ボリビア（南米中部の共和国）」

✲ COMPREHENSION

上のDialogueの内容に関する質問の答えとして適切なものをa～cから選びましょう。

1. Which of the following is true about quinoa?
   a. It is more popular around the world than the potato.
   b. It grows easily in difficult environments and climates.
   c. Though it contains no protein, it is high in other vitamins.

2. Why is Theo worried?
   a. There are too many people in the world and not enough food for them.
   b. Governments in South America are trying to get too much profit from food.
   c. Potatoes should be given more attention and resources than quinoa.

Unit **9** Getting High on Gardening　53

VOCABULARY BUILDING

A 次の太字の語が同じ対比を表すように、空欄に入る適切な語をa～cから選びましょう。

1. **Import** is to **export** as **domestic** is to _____.
   a. international   b. fake   c. profits
2. **Up** is to **down** as _____ is to **basement**.
   a. wall   b. roof   c. door
3. **Eggs** are to **chickens** as _____ are to **farms**.
   a. crops   b. herbicides   c. tools
4. **Macau** is to **Portugal** as _____ is to **China**.
   a. Taiwan   b. Mongolia   c. Hong Kong
5. **Typhoons** are to **Asia** as _____ are to **North America**.
   a. earthquakes   b. hurricanes   c. blizzards

B 文中の下線部の意味を表す語を選びましょう。ただし語は1度しか使えません。

1. _____ My teacher went bananas when I turned in the homework late.
2. _____ When John took his driving test, he was as cool as a cucumber.
3. _____ The girl next door to us is the apple of my eye. I really like her a lot.
4. _____ I wouldn't buy that car if I were you. I'll bet it's a lemon.
5. _____ No wonder Ed wanted to be in the school play. He is such a ham.

> a. calm   b. attractive   c. poor   d. crowded   e. angry
> f. low-quality   g. show-off   h. talkative

Unit 10 The Throw-Away Café!

皆さんの家のアイロンや掃除機、いわゆる電化製品が壊れたとします。新しいのを買わなくても、あなたが1杯のコーヒーか紅茶を飲んでいる間に、機械に詳しい人が壊れたものを直してくれるとしたらどうでしょう。そんな環境に優しい店が現実のものとなったらどうでしょう。そんな店があるのです。その店の人たちは壊れた器具よりも大事なものを直しているのかもしれないのです。

✻ VOCABULARY PREVIEW

次の空欄にあてはまる適切な語を a ～ c から選びましょう。

1. I am going to buy my sister a new _____ for her birthday. She needs a coffee maker, oven, or vacuum cleaner.
   a. produce **b.** outlet **c.** appliance
2. Don't bring your bicycle to the shop. I can _____ your flat tire in a few minutes in my garage.
   a. repair **b.** make **c.** install
3. I want to move to another area in my city. I do not care for this _____ any longer. It has become so dirty and run-down.
   a. lifestyle **b.** neighborhood **c.** spouse
4. My father stopped working last March. He is 65, so he has _____ from his job. He will collect a pension from now on.
   a. quit **b.** hired **c.** retired
5. You should not use so many tissues. They are made out of paper, so you really create a lot of _____.
   a. pleasure **b.** waste **c.** accounting

READING

Imagine that you have just entered a café to have coffee. However, something about this café is different. For example, at the table next to you, a middle-aged woman, holding up an old steam iron, is talking to an elderly
5 man. She is explaining to the white-haired man that the iron no longer works. He listens carefully while sipping his latte. The man then takes the iron from the woman, removes the plastic case, looks inside, and begins removing parts. After working on the iron for ten minutes,
10 he puts the case back on. He plugs it in and pushes the start button. A green light comes on.

The woman smiles, thanks him, finishes her coffee, and leaves with the iron.

Welcome to the Repair Café!

15 The café was started in 2010 in the Netherlands as a way to help people reduce waste. Martine Postma, who founded the café, explains how it started. "I had just had my second child. I was very worried about the environment, and realized that we throw away so many appli-
20 ances and useful things in Europe. Because the world population is increasing, we cannot keep doing this. That is why I opened the café: To do something to help slow down environmental destruction."

This is Postma's business model: The café attracts
25 neighborhood people who have certain skills. For example, one might be good at repairing electrical appliances. Another may be good at sewing. Customers bring their broken coffee makers, washing machines, and torn clothing. One of the volunteer workers at the café then tries
30 to send the mended item back home with the customer for continued use.

Postma asserts that her café is a concrete idea that is beneficial for society in many ways. "We are saving not only goods, but reducing trash. Moreover, my repair-

Notes

steam iron「蒸気アイロン」

latte「ラテ (牛乳にエスプレッソコーヒーを加えた飲み物)」

the Netherlands「オランダ」

electrical appliance「電気器具」

assert「断言する」

people are almost all retired. They are so happy to be contributing to society again. Also, these days, people in neighborhoods seem to know each other less and less. Because of the café, people get to know their neighbors. It has actually helped to rebuild relationships." She smiled. "We are repairing neighborhoods."

The café is good for the economy as well. "Many customers who come to the café cannot afford to have their appliances or goods repaired at ordinary shops," explains Postma. "However, some are not doing poorly; they just think that using the café will help the environment, their neighborhood, or both. My original aim was to reduce the amount of trash in landfills, but this café is pro-consumer, too. When you buy a product, you want to be able to keep it as long as possible. If you don't have to replace it with a new one, you are able to use your money for another service, such as traveling, eating out, or getting a foot massage. We need to build a stronger service economy. This is going to be better for the environment, I think."

Many of us hope to make the world a better place. We take shorter showers, we ride our bicycles to school or work, we use electricity only when necessary, etc. Martine Postma, however, has come up with an innovative idea. Not only is the Repair Café reducing waste, recycling, and reusing, it is bringing isolated people from the neighborhood together while putting the skills of retired people to use again as well.

In short, she is repairing much more than old irons and washing machines. Martine Postma is repairing lives.

✳ COMPREHENSION

英文の内容に関する質問の答えとして適切なものを a ～ c から選びましょう。

1. What was the main reason that Martine Postma opened her café?
    a. She was fed up with the increase in chain coffee shops.
    b. She wanted to create a better world for her daughter.
    c. She did not like seeing unemployed people in her area.
2. Why does she think of her café as pro-consumer?
    a. When people save money on appliances, they use it for a service.
    b. The customers always buy more sweets after trying something.
    c. She pays her workers higher salaries than other cafés do.
3. Which of the following is **not** true about her workers?
    a. Most of them are retired already.
    b. They have different types of skills.
    c. They are paid well for their work.
4. What does Martine Postma imply about building a stronger service economy?
    a. There will be less trash in the landfills.
    b. Travel will improve international relations.
    c. People cook at home too often these days.
5. Why do most people bring something to the café to be repaired?
    a. They believe that the environment is in danger.
    b. It is costly to have something repaired elsewhere.
    c. Improving neighborhood relations is important.

✳ SUMMARY

🎧 DL 030   💿 CD2-30

次の（　）内に、与えられた文字で始まる適切な語を1語ずついれ、音声を聞いて確認しましょう。

　In 2010, Martine Postma opened up a café in ①(H　　　). She had just given ②(b　　) and had become worried about the ③(e　　　).

　Originally, she opened the café to ④(r　　　) the amount of trash Europeans were creating. However, she found that her business model is pro-⑤(c　　　), too. For example, by saving money on a new appliance, that person can purchase a ⑥(s　　　), such as taking a ⑦(t　　　) somewhere.

　She found that her café also ⑧(r　　　) neighborhoods.

　Her business not only addresses the 3Rs, ⑨(r　　　), reusing, and reducing, but it also focuses on an important 4th R: repairing ⑩(l　　　).

DIALOGUE

DL 031　CD2-31

次の会話の音声を聞いて、（　）内に1語ずついれましょう。

(Theo と Rolinda は夕食後に新聞を読んでいます)

T: Wow, Rolinda, you know how you are always telling me to put on a sweater instead of ①(　　　) ②(　　　) the heater? Look at what this guy is doing for the environment!

R: Derreck Kayongo? What has he done?

T: He started collecting soap from hotels. Then he makes new ③(　　　) ④(　　　) soap with this leftover soap.

R: Is that hygienic? I mean, is it safe?

T: It says here that a ⑤(　　　) tests it. When it is declared safe, he sends it out to countries where there is little soap.

R: What a wonderful idea! That must help reduce ⑥(　　　) ⑦(　　　) ⑧(　　　). I once read that soap is a big step toward preventing disease in poor countries.

T: Don't you have some of those small bars of soap from your ⑨(　　　) ⑩(　　　)?

R: I must have more than ⑪(　　　) ⑫(　　　). Let's see if we can find out where to send them. This guy is really doing something great for the environment and people as well.

Notes▶ hygienic「衛生的な」

✳ COMPREHENSION

上のDialogueの内容に関する質問の答えとして適切なものをa〜cから選びましょう。

1. Where did Mr. Kayongo start getting his soap?
    a. He gathered it from countries where there is little soap.
    b. He collected the soap people leave behind in hotels.
    c. He produced luxury soap in his own factories.
2. What does Rolinda probably do on her business trips?
    a. She keeps the soap that is given to her in the hotel.
    b. She always finishes using the soap in her hotel.
    c. She brings back the soap as souvenirs for Theo.

Unit **10** The Throw-Away Café!　59

✳︎✳︎✳︎ VOCABULARY BUILDING

A 次の太字の語が同じ対比を表すように、空欄に入る適切な語を a～c から選びましょう。

1. **Iron** is to **appliance** as **fork** is to _____.
   a. spoon　　　　　　　b. tool　　　　　　　c. utensil
2. **Individual** is to **crowd** as **singular** is to _____.
   a. one　　　　　　　　b. plural　　　　　　c. neighborhood
3. **Retirement** is to **work** as _____ is to **essay**.
   a. conclusion　　　　b. sentence　　　　　c. introduction
4. **Trash** is to **garbage** as **decrease** is to _____.
   a. increase　　　　　b. reduce　　　　　　c. expand
5. **Weather** is to **whether** as **so** is to _____.
   a. sew　　　　　　　　b. sue　　　　　　　　c. saw

B 接頭辞 re- で始まる語が選択肢に並んでいます。1～5 の定義に当たる語を下欄から選び、その記号を空欄に書きましょう。

1. _____ To put more energy into a battery after it has lost or become low on power.
2. _____ To put something to use again after it has been thrown away.
3. _____ To say something again if a person did not understand you.
4. _____ To put up a new house after the old one has been destroyed.
5. _____ To put a new thing in after the old one has become useless.

> a. replace　　b. recycle　　c. recover　　d. recharge
> e. retire　　　f. rebuild　　g. repeat

Unit 11 Lost in Translation?

カナダのケベックを知っていますか。ケベックのまわりには英語を話す人が住んでいるのですが、頑固にフランス文化・言語にこだわり、フランス人からもケベックの人たちのフランス語は Old French と言われているのです。例えば、野球の言葉もすべてフランス語です。英語を借用しないのです。他のどのような分野で政府が英語の侵略に対して戦っていると思いますか…それは買い物なのです。

✲ VOCABULARY PREVIEW

次の空欄にあてはまる適切な語を a〜c から選びましょう。

1. There are so many organizations downtown. Religious, political, and business _____, you will find them all!
   a. establishments **b.** cults **c.** barriers
2. My brother always bothers and harasses me about everything. I wish he would stop _____ me all the time.
   a. caring **b.** bullying **c.** assisting
3. The Japan Society is an important organization, as it promotes Japanese _____ through cultural and artistic events.
   a. heritage **b.** inventions **c.** pesticides
4. Those small shops are not wholesale businesses, but _____. In other words, they sell goods directly to the public.
   a. periodic **b.** organic **c.** retail
5. This novel is not about real life. It is a _____ story. In other words, it was made up.
   a. critical **b.** reproductive **c.** fictitious

READING

When Americans visit Quebec, Canada, they recognize this familiar guy immediately: He is a short, well-dressed, cheerful-looking man with white hair, a neat white beard, and glasses. However, they get confused when they look up and see PFK instead of KFC. Who changed the name of the restaurant? And why?

Laws in Quebec require the name of this fast-food restaurant to be different. Passed in 1977, Quebec's language laws are extremely strict. A business coming to Quebec from another country must change its name to French, or add a sign to explain what it does. Moreover, in their establishments, everything must be in French. For decades, the agency in charge was relaxed about enforcing these laws, but from 2013, it promised to become stricter.

Many within the Canadian government are not happy. "For decades," explains Nathalie St. Pierre, vice-president of the Quebec retail council, "these companies have been doing business with their English names. Everyone knows them. Why does the government suddenly have to bully them? Kentucky Fried Chicken adopted the French name *Poulet Frit Kentucky* many years ago, but what about Pizza Hut, Toys"R"Us, and Best Buy? They have been here for many years, too, only they never took French names. So, what?"

The government has many supporters, however. Martin Bergeron, from the language agency, explained his department's position. "In recent years, so many companies have come into Quebec. Our policy is not anti-American. English, Italian, or Chinese, these businesses have to put out signs in French, or add a sign in French explaining what they do."

Bergeron went on to give an example of how a foreign business could follow the law, using a fictitious company, Daily Living. First, it could change its name to something like *Les Beaux Jours* (The Beautiful Days.) If it did not like this idea, then it could add a French name, much larger than the English one, and put it over the English sign. Or it could add a sign explaining, in French, "Furniture, bedding, and decorations."

"We are just trying to preserve our French language," Mr. Bergeron insists. "We want to serve our French community. We cannot do that if we keep changing everything to English." Quebec is unique in the French-speaking world in that it has preserved a language brought over in the 1600s.

"Look south, east, west, north," Bergeron continues. "We are surrounded by English-speaking people. It is not easy to keep a language that came here hundreds of years ago. Some people say that we are more French than the French. We have to be like that. We have to keep up our heritage, or we will lose it in this global world."

Some think ignoring these laws is acceptable for economic reasons. "Suppose you had a tax law and for years, you did not make anyone pay," says Ms. St. Pierre. "Then suddenly you say, 'OK, now everyone has to pay!' People would find this unfair. It is the same with this language law. What will happen? The government will destroy business in Quebec."

A company with a name in any language other than French will need to obey the laws laid out by the Quebec Office of the French Language. In a world that seems crazy about globalization at every level, it is refreshing to find an island of French in North America that seems to put the preservation of its culture, community, and way of life ahead of money.

✻ COMPREHENSION

英文の内容に関する質問の答えとして適切なものを a ～ c から選びましょう。

1. Mr. Bergeron is worried that:
   a. American businesses will come.   b. Quebec will lose its heritage.
   c. taxes are going to increase.
2. Ms. St. Pierre finds the language laws in Quebec _____.
   a. restrictive   b. important   c. helpful
3. Why did Kentucky Fried Chicken change its name in Quebec?
   a. The company was worried that no one knew Colonel Sanders.
   b. The company decided to comply with the language laws.
   c. The company hoped to create new dishes for Canadian people.
4. Which of the following is **not** true about Quebec?
   a. French has been a mother tongue there for hundreds of years.
   b. The province is surrounded on all sides by English-speakers.
   c. The government is trying hard to keep out foreign companies.
5. How could a foreign company obey the language laws of Quebec?
   a. It could post signs only in its native language, not French.
   b. It could add a sign to its original name, explaining its business.
   c. It could add a small sign in French and put it under its original name.

✻ SUMMARY

DL 033   CD2-41

次の（　）内に、与えられた文字で始まる適切な語を 1 語ずついれ、音声を聞いて確認しましょう。

　Quebec tries very hard to keep its ①(h　　　), its French language and culture. It has many ②(l　　　) to stop English from dominating in Quebec. Since 1977, these ③(s　　　) laws have been in place.

　Many are not happy about this. They believe the laws will ④(d　　　) business in Quebec. As many companies have been there for years with their original names, they think that the ⑤(g　　　) in Quebec is just bullying businesses.

　Many, however, like the law. As Quebec is ⑥(s　　　) by English-speaking people, they find it important to ⑦(p　　　) their French language.

　Basically, there are three ⑧(w　　　) to comply with the law. A company can add a larger sign with a ⑨(t　　　) of its company name in French, it can change its name to French, or it can add a sign ⑩(e　　　) what it does.

DIALOGUE

DL 034 CD2-42

次の会話の音声を聞いて、（　）内に1語ずついれましょう。

（Theo と Rolinda は夕食後に読書をしています）

T: Rolinda, did you know that in Japanese and German, lots of English words are used in baseball? I mean, they use lots of ①(　　　) ②(　　　) such as pitcher and homerun. In Quebec, they don't do that.

R: I don't understand. What do they call a homerun, then?

T: They ③(　　　) two terms for it. Their two expressions for homerun, for example, mean "a circuit of the goals" or "a ④(　　　) ⑤(　　　) four goals." Aren't the Quebecoise so cool, coming up with new words from their old language to protect it and keep foreign words out?

R: I heard that in Iceland, people do something ⑥(　　　). Instead of using the word "computer," as the Japanese do, for example, a new word was created.

T: Wow. How could you ⑦(　　　) ⑧(　　　) with a new word for computer?

R: The government took two existing words, "well" and "knowledge" and combined them to make one word. I read that their language has changed very little since the ⑨(　　　) ⑩(　　　).

T: Language is so interesting. I wonder when English will die out as the global language.

R: It won't be like Latin, Theo. The world has changed a lot since the fifteenth century. English is here to stay.

✷ COMPREHENSION

上の Dialogue の内容に関する質問の答えとして適切なものを a ～ c から選びましょう。

1. Why did the Quebecoise create new words for baseball?
    a. The sport is not played there professionally.
    b. They want to keep their language pure.
    c. They do not want to copy the Japanese.

2. What does Rolinda think about the future of English?
    a. Latin will one day return to replace English as the international language.
    b. It will not be long before English dies out and is replaced by another language.
    c. Global conditions have developed greatly; English will be used from now on.

Unit **11** Lost in Translation?　65

VOCABULARY BUILDING

A 次の太字の語が同じ対比を表すように、空欄に入る適切な語をa～cから選びましょう。

1. **Quebec** is to **French** as **Brazil** is to _____.
   a. Portuguese b. English c. Spanish
2. **Council** is to **counsel** as **idol** is to _____.
   a. hard working b. idle c. hero
3. **Strict** is to **relaxed** as _____ is to **deep**.
   a. depth b. far-reaching c. shallow
4. **Bed** is to _____ as **train** is to **vehicle**.
   a. sleep b. blanket c. furniture
5. **South** is to _____ as **six** is to **watch**.
   a. compass b. thermometer c. north

B 次は何の略語でしょうか。次の空欄にあてはまる適切な語をa～cから選びましょう。

1. F.B.I.: The Federal Bureau of _____
   a. Institution b. Illegality c. Investigation
2. W.H.O.: The _____ Health Organization
   a. Whole b. World c. Wealthy
3. N.B.A.: The National Basketball _____
   a. Agency b. Athletics c. Association
4. N.A.T.O.: The North Atlantic _____ Organization
   a. Treaty b. Trust c. Truce
5. P.M.: Post _____
   a. Morning b. Middle c. Meridian

Unit 12　The Very Fortunate Four

「努力は必ず報われます。一生懸命やれば名声もついてきます」とはよく耳にする言葉です。もちろん努力は大事ですが、もう一つ大事な要素が見過ごされています。それは「運」です。有名になった人は、その人のある時期の「運」に助けられ、名声を得たと述懐しています。この課に登場する男性グループは単に普通の奴らだと見過ごされていたかもしれないのです。彼らに「運」がなかったら。彼らとはさて誰でしょう？

✲ VOCABULARY PREVIEW

次の空欄にあてはまる適切な語を a 〜 c から選びましょう。

1. Though unemployment went down in 2014, most of the new jobs were added in the fast-food _____.
   a. obstacle　　　　**b.** industry　　　　**c.** complexity
2. If you have a good suggestion about using the campus gymnasium in the evenings, please submit a _____ to the dean of students.
   a. contract　　　　**b.** disguise　　　　**c.** proposal
3. That university is among the best three in the country. It is very _____.
   a. prestigious　　　**b.** mediocre　　　　**c.** unreliable
4. 12 companies have turned me down already. I cannot handle one more _____.
   a. acceptance　　　**b.** emergence　　　**c.** rejection
5. While a director often works on the artistic points of a film or album, the _____ usually handles the monetary or financial aspects of the project.
   a. actor　　　　　　**b.** producer　　　　**c.** janitor

READING

Brian Epstein was excited. The lunchtime performance at the club was nearly over, but he had to get back to his record store. He really liked the band he had just seen. Although he had no experience as a manager, he asked the four boys if he could represent them.

They agreed, but Epstein soon discovered that finding jobs for them was hard. Many thought of them as unreliable and arrogant. Epstein tried to arrange a recording for them at Decca, a company that was very prestigious in the music industry. The company, however, rejected them. "You have a good record business," a Decca representative advised Epstein. "Stick to that and forget these guys. They are going nowhere."

The group thought it was finished. The young men were very disappointed by this rejection, which was actually their second. EMI, the largest company in England at the time, had rejected them first.

Epstein was not ready to give up just yet. He went to every record company he could find; each and every one turned down the group. After that, he returned to EMI with a new tape. A producer named George Martin listened to it. "The songs are not very good," he confessed to Epstein.

This might have been the end of the story, but Epstein managed to get two colleagues of Martin's interested in the band. They had a proposal to make. Sid Colman, one of the two, suggested that he pay for a recording. This was highly unusual. So the band returned to EMI and made a record. Not only did the two fail to persuade their company to put out the record, but their colleagues called the band's name ridiculous.

Epstein had come close to helping the boys put out a record. Using his own money, he bought the single record the group had recorded, a song called "Love Me Do."

Notes

arrogant「横柄な」

EMI = Electrical and Musical Industries の略（英国のレコード会社）

turn down〜「〜を断る」

colleague「同僚」

ridiculous「ばかばかしい」

35 He made use of the group's fan base in Liverpool and pushed the record along. It caught the interest of many and became a hit. Though George Martin liked neither the group nor the song, he grudgingly became their producer. If they had had a hit with this song, then perhaps
40 they could have more; his business sense had prevailed over his personal tastes.

Martin now had to let the group have a second chance. This time, he asked two of the members to write all of the songs. They did. EMI released the record, and
45 it became an enormous hit.

The most interesting part of this story is the chain of events that led to the group's success. What if Brian Epstein had never pushed for the group? What if Sid Colman had not risked his own money to produce a re-
50 cord? What if EMI had never asked them to come back? Finally, imagine if Epstein had just let the record recording fail.

This is often how success happens in life. We might never have listened to any of their songs, but thanks to
55 many people behind the scenes, this group became famous. Their success was not destiny, it was the result of hard work… and luck.

Moreover, had all of these people behind the scenes not pushed so hard, perhaps nobody would know the "ri-
60 diculous" name of the group: The Beatles.

Billy Hatton said this in a recent documentary film: "Many people say, 'Oh, we knew the Beatles were going to be successful from the beginning!' This just was not true. Nobody saw the Beatles' success coming… nobody."

Notes

grudgingly「いやいやで」

prevail over ~「~に打ち勝つ」

behind the scenes「舞台裏で」
destiny「運命」

✲ COMPREHENSION

英文の内容に関する質問の答えとして適切なものをa〜cから選びましょう。

1. What does Mr. Hatton imply in a documentary film in 2014?
   a. Luck played a very strong part in the success of the Beatles.
   b. The Beatles had no chance to succeed from the beginning.
   c. Except for Mr. Hatton, nobody knew that the Beatles would succeed.
2. What is true about George Martin, the Beatles' producer?
   a. He never gave up on them after seeing them during a lunch break.
   b. Though he never really liked their music, he felt they might succeed.
   c. He used the fan base in Liverpool to make the group very popular.
3. How did Sid Colman contribute to the success of the Beatles?
   a. He substituted on the drums for Ringo Starr from time to time.
   b. He persuaded everyone in his company that their name was fine.
   c. He put up his own money to help the Beatles make a recording.
4. Which record company turned the group down first?
   a. EMI   b. Decca   c. Apple
5. After agreeing to be the manager of the Beatles, what did Brian Epstein find?
   a. Everyone in England was crazy about the Beatles.
   b. It was difficult to find jobs for them anywhere.
   c. Many record companies hoped to sign them.

✲ SUMMARY

DL 036　CD2-54

次の（　）内に、与えられた文字で始まる適切な語を1語ずつ入れ、音声を聞いて確認しましょう。

　　Though it would seem that the Beatles were certain to ①(s　　　　), luck played a great part in their fate. Thanks to the hard work of many, the Beatles were able to put out a record with a ②(p　　　　) company.

　　Brian Epstein, their ③(m　　　　), may have been the most important person for the Beatles. He had a ④(r　　　　) store, but he tried hard to promote the four men. After they were ⑤(r　　　　) by two famous record companies, he refused to ⑥(g　　　　) up on them. Ultimately, he ⑦(b　　　　) their recording with his own money and used their fan base in Liverpool to create a hit.

　　Although their ⑧(p　　　　), George Martin, cared little for their music, he had a ⑨(h　　　　) that they would succeed ⑩(f　　　　).

DIALOGUE

DL 037　CD2-55

次の会話の音声を聞いて、（　）内に1語ずついれましょう。

（Theo と Rolinda は夕食後に読書をしています）

T: Wow… Rolinda, we talked about how much luck the Beatles had, but ①(　　　) ②(　　　) ③(　　　). I am reading about "The 27 Club."

R: What is that, a new band?

T: No… there must be more than 50 musicians on this list, all who died at the age of 27. For example, Brian Jones was in the Rolling Stones. He ④(　　　) in 1969. Then three famous rock stars died from problems with drugs and alcohol: Jim Morrison, Jimi Hendrix, and Janis Joplin.

R: Gosh, I have heard of all of them. Are there any more ⑤(　　　) cases?

T: Sure. Do you remember Amy Winehouse? She died in ⑥(　　　) from alcohol poisoning.

R: I wonder why I never heard of this club before.

T: It says that Kurt Cobain, who committed ⑦(　　　) at 27, made it famous. His mother had told him, "Don't join that 27 club!"

R: Why do they die so young, when they are so successful and probably rich?

T: There were car accidents and some murders, but most of them seem to be related to drugs.

R: Maybe artists live wild lives. Or maybe ⑧(　　　) and big ⑨(　　　) are hard to handle for a young person.

Notes▶ wild life「放縦な生活」

✴ COMPREHENSION

上の Dialogue の内容に関する質問の答えとして適切なものを a～c から選びましょう。

1. Which is **not** a common characteristic among the members of *The 27 Club*?
    a. They were murdered.　　b. They died at the age of 27.
    c. They were artists.
2. What does Rolinda suggest at the end of the dialogue?
    a. It is hard for a young artist to handle life as a famous person.
    b. There is too much drug and alcohol abuse among the young.
    c. It is odd that many rock stars still tour in their 60s and 70s.

Unit **12**　The Very Fortunate Four

✳✳✳ VOCABULARY BUILDING

A 次の太字の語が同じ対比を表すように、空欄に入る適切な語を a～c から選びましょう。

1. **Song** is to **album** as _____ is to **book**.
   a. sentence **b.** preface **c.** chapter
2. **Rhythm** is to **poetry** as _____ is to **music**.
   a. audience **b.** tempo **c.** melody
3. **Camera** is to **photographer** as _____ is to **musician**.
   a. instrument **b.** tool **c.** utensil
4. **Night** is to **day** as _____ is to **accept**.
   a. reject **b.** except **c.** agree
5. **Unreliable** is to **dependable** as **arrogant** is to _____.
   a. egotistic **b.** narcissistic **c.** modest

B 音楽に関わる慣用表現です。次の空欄にあてはまる適切な語を a～c から選びましょう。

1. Professor Higgens wants to talk to you about your test. Your score must have been pretty bad. You had better go into his office and _____.
   a. blow your horn **b.** face the music **c.** ring his bells
2. You invited Jane to the party, now you say she is not invited? Wow, you have really _____.
   a. danced at two weddings **b.** changed your tune **c.** rung her bell
3. I am not sure whether we will keep driving to Chicago or stop in a small town and rest. Let's _____.
   a. face the music **b.** pick up the beat **c.** play it by ear
4. I think I have met Dan somewhere before. His face really _____.
   a. rings a bell **b.** plays it by ear **c.** rocks the house
5. Are you really going to pay me back the money you borrowed last year? That's _____.
   a. fine tuning **b.** rhythm and soul **c.** music to my ears

Unit 13

Health, a Salty Reality

過去20年の間、医学界の定説の虚偽がいくつか暴かれてきました。医者は1日に何リットルかの水分は必要だと言っていましたが、今や多くの医者がその必要はないと言っています。この課では減塩食を取り上げます。過去20年、皆さんが減塩食に熱心に取り組んでいなかったことを願って。(実際そうする必要はなかったようです…)

✳ VOCABULARY PREVIEW

次の空欄にあてはまる適切な語を a～c から選びましょう。

1. My mother always prepares dishes from scratch, using fresh food. She never uses frozen or _____ food. She doesn't like food that was treated with chemicals.
   a. raw **b.** processed **c.** organic

2. I am not going to live in the dormitory forever. It is just my _____ home.
   a. permanent **b.** eternal **c.** temporary

3. My mother told me to put ice on my injured shoulder, but my father gave me _____ advice: He told me to use a heat pad.
   a. strict **b.** contradictory **c.** prestigious

4. After an elderly person has a _____, it is often difficult for that person to move parts of his or her body.
   a. cough **b.** fever **c.** stroke

5. The _____ on space exploration is going to give us a report next Tuesday. Then we will know if the astronauts will be traveling to space or not.
   a. earnings **b.** committee **c.** reservation

READING

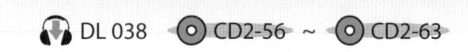

    50 years ago, children were likely to hear advice such as this: Get lots of sunshine, eat red meat frequently, and use margarine, not butter. Today, such suggestions might seem puzzling or open to debate. Coffee is another puzzle. For years, doctors warned that it was terrible for a person's health. Then, not long ago, coffee showed up on a list of food/beverages that doctors strongly recommended for preventing cancer.

    Opinions and advice in the world of health change all the time. Have there been any recent shifts in opinion? The low-salt diet is one. Until a few years ago, doctors recommended no more than a half teaspoon of salt per day. This was thought to be helpful in reducing the risk of heart attacks or strokes.

    In 2013, however, a prestigious health committee announced that there is no reason to cut down sodium consumption or to follow a low-salt diet. This might puzzle those in the United States, where for years many packages have been labeled, "Low in Sodium! Low in Salt!"

    The group that made this announcement was formed by the CDCP, or Center for Disease Control and Prevention. Its report may confuse people who were told not to consume more than 1500 milligrams of sodium a day. According to the report, a person should not consume below 2300 milligrams a day. On the contrary, the group found that a person has a higher risk of heart attack if he or she goes below that level. These recommendations are contradictory to what people have been told for the past several decades.

    The committee talked more about salt and sodium as they relate to health in general. It came to the conclusion that there should be no limit on sodium consumption. It stated in a vague way that a person should try not to eat too much salt. However, its report is far more

Notes

puzzling「わけが分からない」
open to debate「さらに議論が必要な」
puzzle「なぞ」

low-salt diet「減塩ダイエット」

heart attack「心臓発作」
stroke「脳卒中」

sodium consumption「ナトリウム消費量」

milligram = 1/1000 gram

on the contrary「それどころか」

come to the conclusion that ~「～という結論に達する」

detailed and clear about the opposite situation. The problem with too little sodium in the diet is this: Triglyceride levels increase, insulin resistance increases, and the activity of the nervous system increases. All of these are dangerous to the heart.

Some doctors are not ready to change their minds on this important issue. They believe it will cause problems for the public. "This report will send this message to people: You can eat as much salt as you like. This just isn't right," explains Bonnie Liebman, Director of Nutrition at the Center for Science in the Public Interest. The American Heart Association agrees. Processed food in America is high in sodium, which makes a large cut in sodium almost impossible. Processed food has become a central part of many Americans' diets; these foods are high in both salt and sodium.

The Center for Disease Control and Prevention stands by its findings. The major problem with earlier research, the center says, is that scientists looked too hard for connections between what people ate and their health. The CDCP insists, however, that researchers need to consider many other factors. For example, how much does a person exercise? This factor alone will affect his or her salt/sodium consumption levels.

As research moves ahead, new findings are sure to come out on many subjects. The low-salt diet is the latest advice to come into question. What will be next? As Isaac Newton said hundreds of years ago, all knowledge is temporary and should be open to doubt and revision. In the world of health, this seems to be very true.

✱ COMPREHENSION

英文の内容に関する質問の答えとして適切なものを a ～ c から選びましょう。

1. What was the problem with early research on salt in the diet?
    a. The research relied too much on the connection between diet and health only.
    b. The research focused on people with health problems in lower income groups.
    c. The research was supported with funding from the National Salt Association.
2. Bonnie Liebman worried about the report because people will:
    a. misunderstand the results.   b. be free to eat lots of salt.
    c. get angry at her committee.
3. What will happen if a person consumes too little sodium?
    a. The person will get excellent results on his or her physical examination.
    b. A person's nervous system may become overly active, causing a heart attack.
    c. A person will be likely to consume excessive amounts of water.
4. What criticism did the CDCP have for American people in general?
    a. Their consumption of alcohol has reached dangerous levels.
    b. Red meat and margarine need to be eaten more frequently.
    c. The average person's diet contains too much processed food.
5. Why has the report caused confusion among people?
    a. The information is contradictory to that given over the past three decades.
    b. The report calls for an increase in sodium, but a sharp decrease in salt.
    c. Most doctors believe that the research in the report has been falsified.

✱ SUMMARY   DL 039 CD2-64

次の（　）内に、与えられた文字で始まる適切な語を1語ずついれ、音声を聞いて確認しましょう。

　In 2013, a report was released by a ①(c　　　) from the Center for Disease Control and Prevention. In the report, it was announced that a low salt, low ②(s　　　) diet is actually not good for people. These findings were ③(c　　　) to what people had heard from doctors in previous ④(d　　　).

　Not all doctors ⑤(a　　　) with the report. Some believe that people will ⑥(m　　　) it, and health problems will increase. Also, the American Heart Association would like to see American people eat less ⑦(p　　　) food.

　People who eat too little sodium are at a high ⑧(r　) of suffering a ⑨(h　) attack. Also, the CDCP urged doctors to take ⑩(e　　　) into consideration.

DIALOGUE

次の会話の音声を聞いて、（　）内に1語ずついれましょう。

（Theo と Rolinda は夕食後に新聞を読んでいます）

T: So many things we do are going to change in the future, Rolinda. You used a travel agent to plan our vacation the other day, for example. There won't be any in 20 years, I bet.

R: You might be right. A person is going to be able to plan a trip on the computer. What about that newspaper you are reading? I heard that ①(　　　) ②(　　　　), newspapers will no longer exist in paper form.

T: I'm not ③(　　　) ④(　　　　) ⑤(　　　) that. I guess I will have to bring a book with me when I commute to work. And what about watches? I wonder if anybody will wear them any more.

R: I think ⑥(　　　　) will, but it seems that people will always like them as jewelry. But to tell time, most people are probably going to use their ⑦(　　　) ⑧(　　　　).

T: Oh … the world changes too fast. Let's listen to some music, Rolinda. I just got this really good CD.

R: OK … but you don't need that disc in your hand. I ⑨(　　　　　) the same CD just last week

T: Progress… sometimes I just want to say enough is enough.

Notes ▸ commute to work「通勤する」　enough is enough「もうたくさんだ」

✳ COMPREHENSION

上のDialogueの内容に関する質問の答えとして適切なものをa～cから選びましょう。

1. What does Rolinda think will happen to watches in the future?
   a. Few will be bought because people will use cell phones to tell time.
   b. Fewer of them will be bought, but they will have fashion appeal.
   c. Electricity may become scarce so more people will buy them.
2. According to the story, when does Theo usually read the newspaper?
   a. On his way to work.　　**b.** At breakfast.　　**c.** In the library.

Unit **13** Health, a Salty Reality

✱✱ VOCABULARY BUILDING

A 次の太字の語が同じ対比を表すように、空欄に入る適切な語をa～cから選びましょう。

1. **Margarine** is to **butter** as **saccharine** is to _____.
   a. coffee b. meat c. sugar
2. **Stress** is to **heart attack** as **sunshine** is to _____.
   a. stroke b. Alzheimer's disease c. skin cancer
3. _____ is to **natural** as **processed** is to **organic**.
   a. artificial b. consumption c. taste
4. _____ is to **organization** as **Wednesday** is to **week**.
   a. entity b. committee c. goal
5. **Warning** is to _____ as **fiction** is to **fact**.
   a. suggestion b. trouble c. consideration

B 医師と話すときに使われる表現です。下線部の語(句)に当たる適切なものをa～cから選びましょう。

1. I am going to check your heart beat. <u>Inhale</u> deeply and hold it.
   a. bend over b. breathe in c. raise your arm
2. How much alcohol do you <u>consume</u> in a week?
   a. take in b. purchase c. put out
3. You need to <u>reduce</u> the amount of sugar you eat every day.
   a. raise b. lower c. eliminate
4. I'm afraid that your <u>cardiovascular activity</u> is a bit down. You will need to exercise more.
   a. breathing b. blood flow c. thought process
5. You are going to need to <u>refrain from</u> smoking if you want to get over this infection.
   a. increase b. stop c. reduce

Unit 14 First the Mammoth, Next the Elephant?

トラ、ライオン、クマなど絶滅の危機に瀕する動物は多いのです。この状況を食い止めることは可能に思えますが、我々人間はどうもこのような生き物たちを根絶するという欲望を払拭できないようです。リョコウバトはかつてアメリカで何十億羽と生存していましたが、1914年には絶滅してしまいました。私たちの祖先によって絶滅させられた動物たちを見てみましょう。

✳ VOCABULARY PREVIEW

次の空欄にあてはまる適切な語を a～c から選びましょう。

1. It will probably never be known for certain why dinosaurs became _____. There are many theories about how they disappeared from this planet.
    a. abundant　　　b. extinct　　　c. numerous
2. Because of the terrible disease affecting them, all of the cows in the herd had to be _____. Killing so many animals at once was a terrible shame.
    a. slaughtered　　　b. bred　　　c. nurtured
3. Who took the pen from my desk? I can't wait to find out who the _____ is.
    a. victim　　　b. physician　　　c. culprit
4. Because many of the _____ in Minnesota came from Sweden, Finland, and Norway, the influence of Scandinavian heritage is very strong there.
    a. settlers　　　b. vandals　　　c. accountants
5. Bats give birth to their babies, they do not lay eggs. They are _____.
    a. reptiles　　　b. amphibians　　　c. mammals

READING

    10,000 years ago, North America was home to many large mammals, more than are found in Africa today. Giant sloths were plentiful. Another common mammal was the wooly mammoth, an elephant covered with heavy fur. There were also hairy rhinoceroses. There were millions upon millions of all of these, but then there were suddenly none. What happened?

    After years of research, scientists may have found the culprit: the Clovis, the earliest settlers in North America. The Clovis, many scientists believe, wandered over to the American continent during an Ice Age. They spread out all over North America once they had arrived from Asia.

    At 14 sites throughout North America, many, many skeletons of the giant sloth, the wooly mammoth, and other creatures from that time period were found along with the points of Clovis spears. It seems that humans had acquired the skills to hunt these large plant-eating animals. How did such a small number of humans get rid of millions of very large animals?

    Some scientists believe it was the weather, or over-chill. At the end of the Pleistocene era, just as glaciers were melting away, the world may have experienced a short Ice Age. This could have sent temperatures down or up in certain areas. This extreme change in temperatures may have killed off many large mammals.

    Over-ill is another possibility. Human diseases in North America may have spread to animals. The weather could have helped. For example, frozen waterways could have allowed migrants to walk over from Asia, bringing sicknesses along with them. Again, the Clovis could have been the culprits. Warming, too, might have created conditions by which diseases easily spread.

    However, most scientists now believe over-kill was the cause. Our ancestors simply hunted these easy targets, which were slow and harmless to humans, into extinction. Many of the skeleton bones were found where water holes existed. It was easy for humans to wait for the animals there.

In the 1800s, the same thing happened to passenger pigeons. They stuck together in the same trees, allowing hunters to kill them by the thousands at one time. People killed them not only for food and other products, but for enjoyment. By 1914, this species, which had numbered in the billions just two centuries before, was extinct.

The buffalo and bison of the North American plains were nearly wiped out as well. However such slaughter was not limited to the past. In Africa, by the 1980s, half of its elephants had been killed, mostly for ivory. In Chad, for example, there were still 4,350 elephants in 2002. Today, there are about 450. This slaughter continues now, as you read this.

Scientist Paul Martin blames humans alone for this situation. "In my lifetime, millions of people were slaughtered, from Europe's Jewish population in the Holocaust to entire populations of minority groups in Darfur. This is proof of what humans are capable of. Why did humans get rid of wooly mammoths in the Pleistocene era? Because they could. Why did Americans get rid of the passenger pigeons? No one stopped to think about the consequences. Could the same happen to elephants? Tigers? Mountain lions? Bears? US?"

Many groups of animals that you know today may not make it to the twenty-second century… or small numbers of them may exist only in zoos. Development, environmental destruction, and human egotism may result in disaster. Many of the world's species seem to be going the way of the mammoth.

✳ COMPREHENSION

英文の内容に関する質問の答えとして適切なものを a～c から選びましょう。

1. About how many of the elephants in Chad have been killed in recent years?
   a. 10% **b.** 50% **c.** 90%
2. Which of the following did **not** go extinct in North America?
   a. The passenger pigeon. **b.** The mammoth. **c.** The buffalo.
3. What wiped out the large mammals of North America roughly 9000 years ago?
   a. Over-chill. **b.** Over-ill. **c.** Over-kill.
4. How did weather help destroy the large mammals in North America?
   a. It helped to create ways for humans to enter North America.
   b. It drove people to kill animals in order to get fur for clothing.
   c. It dried up all of the sources of water for people and animals.
5. What will happen to many species of wild animals in the future?
   a. Much of the world will be turned into a zoo.
   b. Many of the species will become extinct.
   c. Humans will change and save most animals.

✳ SUMMARY

🎧 DL 042   ◎ CD2-76

次の（　）内に、与えられた文字で始まる適切な語を1語ずつ入れ、音声を聞いて確認しましょう。

　Elephants are now in danger of becoming ①(e　　　　) in Africa. This is difficult to stop, as hunters kill them for their ②(i　　　　) and other reasons that bring them money. However, simple ③(d　　　　) threatens many other species such as tigers, bears, and mountain lions. As humans increase, there will be less space for animals.

　Throughout history, humans have wiped out entire ④(s　　　　) of animals. Scientists have discovered that this probably happened to large ⑤(m　　　　) about 9000 years ago, such as the wooly mammoth and giant sloth. Our ancestors killed them at watering holes, using ⑥(s　　　　).

　In more modern times, the passenger ⑦(p　　　　) was driven into extinction. These harmless birds were killed for food, to make clothing, and simply for ⑧(e　　　　). By the year 2100, many animals will exist only in ⑨(z　　　　). The rest will likely be killed off due to ⑩(e　　　　) destruction, development, and human egotism.

DIALOGUE

DL 043　CD2-77

次の会話の音声を聞いて、（　）内に1語ずついれましょう。

（Theo と Rolinda は夕食後に新聞を読んでいます）

T: Rolinda, according to this article, the Japanese eel is one of the species at risk of ①(　　　　　).

R: Oh, no! Theo, eel is your favorite food! Does the article say how bad the situation is?

T: Well, in 1980, 1,920 tons of eel ②(　　　　　) ③(　　　　　). In 2011, just 229 tons were. This is not the worst news, however. Juvenile eels are down 90%.

R: That means there are far fewer young eels available to ④(　　　　　).

T: Well, that is it. No more eel for dinner. I think that we should have vegetarian meals ⑤(　　　) ⑥(　　　　　) three nights a week.

R: I wondered why eel had become so expensive. I heard that the same thing is happening with scallops. Development has had a bad effect on their natural habitats.

T: Do you think that Japanese people can cut their ⑦(　　　　　) of eel?

R: I doubt that. But I hope the government will think of restricting eel fishing and work on ⑧(　　　　　) with other governments in the area.

Notes▶ at risk「危険な状態に」　juvenile「十分生育していない」　scallop「ホタテガイ」　I doubt that.「それは疑わしい」

✳ COMPREHENSION

上の Dialogue の内容に関する質問の答えとして適切なものを a～c から選びましょう。

1. How large has the decrease been in the number of eels caught in the past three decades?
   a. 16%　　**b.** 63%　　**c.** 88%
2. What is one reason that the number of eels has decreased?
   a. Human development has been too extensive.
   b. Scallops have taken over areas once inhabited by eels.
   c. The price of eel in Japan has increased in recent years.

Unit **14**　First the Mammoth, Next the Elephant?　83

VOCABULARY BUILDING

A 次の太字の語が同じ対比を表すように、空欄に入る適切な語をa～cから選びましょう。

1. **Mammoth** is to **elephant** as _____ is to **human**.
    a. female   b. mammal   c. ape
2. **Species** is to _____ as **swing** is to **jazz**.
    a. family   b. genus   c. category
3. **Fur** is to **body** as _____ is to **bed**.
    a. blanket   b. ceiling   c. pillow
4. **Acquire** is to **abandon** as **cause** is to _____.
    a. consequence   b. reason   c. extinction
5. **Kill** is to **slaughter** as **laugh** is to _____.
    a. roar   b. smile   c. chuckle

B 次の空欄にあてはまる適切な語をa～cから選びましょう。

1. My brother-in-law studies the origins of words. He is an _____.
    a. optometrist   b. etymologist   c. archaeologist
2. My niece studies human culture, society, and its development. She is a(n): _____
    a. botanist   b. physicist   c. anthropologist
3. My nephew is a doctor who takes care of only children. He is a: _____
    a. geriatrician   b. dietician   c. pediatrician
4. My uncle knows every insect in the woods because he is an _____.
    a. entomologist   b. astronomer   c. ornithologist
5. My grandfather studied the religions of the world. He was a _____.
    a. theologian   b. genealogist   c. zoologist

Unit 15
Battling the Blues

有名人のサインをもらったり、握手をしたことはありますか。どんな感じであったかその時のことを覚えていますか。そのような経験がなければ、想像してみて下さい。これから読んでもらう物語は、ニューヨークでのある有名な男性ミュージシャンとの出会いを描いたものです。でも、この物語にはちょっとした「オチ」があります。それは何でしょう。

✳ VOCABULARY PREVIEW

次の空欄にあてはまる適切な語を a〜c から選びましょう。

1. My wife _____ me on my new outfit, which made me happy. I had spent a lot of time choosing it at the department store.
   a. complimented **b.** scolded **c.** ignored

2. "I am afraid I have some very bad news. We have all just lost our jobs!" Steve said to me with a _____ look on his face.
   a. pleasant **b.** cheerful **c.** solemn

3. My brother-in-law pretended he was a business executive. He had made up that story just to impress everyone. Actually, he was just an _____ who left home every day in a suit, but changed into his uniform at the fast food restaurant where he worked.
   a. entertainer **b.** imposter **c.** autograph

4. My sister's son is always causing trouble when he comes over. However, he never does any serious damage; he is just a typical, _____ four-year-old boy.
   a. elegant **b.** fearful **c.** mischievous

5. Though John's mother will not allow him to go abroad this summer, John is still _____ with his parents over their decision.
   a. battling **b.** despairing **c.** grinning

READING

My wife and I were early for a dinner appointment at a friend's house in New York City one spring night, so we decided to stop by an elegant café to have a drink. It looked expensive. We sat at a small table near a large window and ordered. Then I noticed that the workers were talking in hushed, excited tones about a man at the end of the bar. "He's here again!" one whispered. Another waiter hurried over. "Here is your martini, Mr. Chambers!" The customer smiled and gave him a slight, graceful bow. The customer was very fashionably dressed.

A blonde woman passed by the charming man. "Say," he exclaimed in a rather loud voice, "you remind me of Grace Kelly!" He told another woman that she looked like a famous actress. They both smiled and thanked the elderly gentleman. Usually, I thought, this behavior would not be acceptable. However, nobody seemed to mind as Mr. Chambers drank, talked, and paid compliments to any woman who passed. He seemed to be a regular at this café.

My wife and I enjoyed our drinks quietly. My second cocktail had slid down smoothly, so I ordered a third. Just then, I overheard Mr. Chambers say to the bartender, "Today? Oh, I played chess in Central Park this morning with Ornette." "And how is Mr. Hollander, sir?" replied the bartender. "Oh, he's doin' OK, but like me, we're not getting it on *on* the stage, we are just getting *on* in the years!" He chuckled and threw up his hands as the bartender laughed along politely at this puzzling attempt at humor.

I said to my wife in a whisper, "He played chess with Ornette HOLLANDER?"

"Who is he?" asked my wife. I was surprised.

"What? He is probably the most famous saxophone player ever!" As a great fan of jazz, I had to go over and talk to Mr. Chambers. I rose from my seat and walked to the end of the bar. "Excuse me, sir, but could I buy you a drink?"

He invited me to sit down, and we began chatting away. While telling a story, without even a slight pause, he winked at a woman who had just walked in the bar. My wife joined us and listened to Mr. Chambers go on about his trips to Europe, his tours in Asia, Charlie Parker, Charles Mingus, Miles Davis… he knew everyone who was famous in the world of jazz.

Then I told him, "Mr. Chambers, *River Pearls* is my favorite number!" It had been Roman Chambers' biggest hit. He put down his drink slowly and solemnly shook my hand. "You know music, my man! Yes, sir, you sure do know your music!"

My wife whispered that we were late for our dinner appointment. "I hope I am not being rude, Mr. Chambers, but I am just a big, big fan of yours. Could I contact you again… and maybe buy you lunch?" Sure, he said, as he flipped me an elegant-looking name card. I could not believe it. I had the name card and contact information of one of the greatest musicians of all time. And I was going to have lunch with him! Just the two of us!

He was grinning and raising his eyebrows at a young, pretty woman who had just come in. Another customer from the bar moved next to Chambers to take my place.

At dinner that night, all I could talk about was Roman Chambers. My friends were amazed. "You know people in high places now!" Bill, my best friend, joked. "Are you sure that you still want to be friends with me?" "Did you get his autograph?" asked Bill's wife. I explained that our meeting had not been like that. "It wasn't like meeting somebody really famous. It was different. We were like… I don't know, it was like we were friends or some-

---

Notes

flip「ぽいっと投げる」

of all time「古今を通じてまれに見る」

grin「にこっと笑う」
raise one's eyebrows「眉を上げる」

in high places「上流社会」

Unit 15 Battling the Blues 87

thing," I explained.

That night, I could not sleep. After getting out of bed, I turned on my computer so that I could read up on the great Roman Chambers. I opened up a page on the Internet. Then I got an incredible shock.

The man in the bar had been slender, maybe 70 years old at most. According to the Internet page, the overweight Roman Chambers was born in 1906... and had died in 2002! Had he been alive, Mr. Chambers would have been over 100! It would have been unlikely to find such a man in a drinking establishment alone or as active as that man in the bar.

I looked through my wallet. I found Mr. Chambers' card. There was no e-mail address on it. Though it was very late, I phoned the number. "I am sorry," said a recorded voice. "The number you have reached has either been disconnected or is out of order." I frowned.

What was going on?

I went back to the bar many times after that night. The staff said that Mr. Chambers had come in many times during the past half year, but he had not come in again since the night he met me. I thought it over again and again and then came to an angry realization: I had not met Roman Chambers. I had met an imposter!

Several months later, I stopped by a luxurious little hotel in Greenwich Village to have a nightcap with Bill. As I sat down, I looked over at a table where three people were engaged in a lively discussion. Sure enough, there he was: Roman Chambers! He was dressed differently, somewhat academic, but it was definitely him.

"Bill, can you give me a minute? I will be right back!" I said, and headed towards Chambers' table.

He saw me approaching. His eyes were fixed on mine. Clearly, he remembered me.

Notes

read up on ~「~を（読んで）徹底的に研究する」

incredible「信じられない」

at most「せいぜい」

Had he been alive = If he had been alive

frown「顔をしかめる」

Greenwich Village「グリニッジビレッジ（NY市のマンハッタンの特に若い芸術家の集まる地区）」
nightcap「寝酒」
be engaged in a lively discussion「活発な論議を戦わす」

"Well, well, ROMAN Chambers!" I exclaimed, spreading my arms out in the air. As I stared into his eyes, I saw a basketful of emotions: Despair, desperation, fear, and then more.

Just then, one of the two men at his table said, "Uh, sorry, you are making a mistake. This is Edward Hawkins, the novelist!" For a long moment, I stared into those eyes. Now they flashed anxiety. 'What are you going to do?' the eyes seemed to ask me. An uncomfortable pause followed.

"Of course!" I exclaimed suddenly, guffawing loudly. "Mr. Hawkins, I love your work. You know, you do look a lot like Roman Chambers, but how silly of me… he passed away more than a decade ago!"

The elderly man stood, pressed his hand into mine, and covered it with his other hand. Then he said slowly, "Thank you, son, thank you SO MUCH for this honor!" His eyes now flashed relief and gratitude. I caught deep warmth in them as well. He gave me a sad, but thankful smile.

Before going to bed that night, I thought about what had happened. Had I done the right thing? Which is better, an elderly man sitting alone in his apartment at night, or that same man having harmless, mischievous fun, deceiving people out in public? He was not an artist, most likely, or at least, he was not a famous one. However, he had brightened our lives for just one night. It was all so strange. Did that old man just want to feel special? Did he enjoy seeing us feel special? Was his lie a creative way of battling loneliness and old age?

His performances had brightened my life, in any case. I had that to thank him for. Satisfied that there was enough truth in that, I switched off the light to embrace the solitude of the blues.

Notes

basketful 「かなりの量の」

flash anxiety 「不安が顔を横切る」

guffaw~ 「～を馬鹿笑いする」

pass away 「死ぬ」

in any case 「ともかく」

⁜ COMPREHENSION

英文の内容に関する質問の答えとして適切なものをａ～ｃから選びましょう。

1. Which of the following is most likely true about the elderly man?
  a. He had once been a great musician who toured all over the world.
  b. Women loved him because he had written several great novels.
  c. He was acting like a famous person to fight off loneliness.

2. The couple in this story went into an elegant bar to:
  a. meet a famous person. **b.** kill time before a party.
  c. discuss a story with a writer.

3. How did Bill react that night when his friend told him about Roman Chambers?
  a. He was jealous. **b.** He joked about it. **c.** He asked for his autograph.

4. The waiters at the café were excited because they thought:
  a. a famous jazz artist was there. **b.** tips would be high.
  c. few customers had come.

5. Most likely, why couldn't the narrator sleep after meeting Roman Chambers?
  a. He was angry that an imposter had deceived him.
  b. He was unhappy with the meal at his friend's house.
  c. He was excited about meeting a famous person.

⁜ SUMMARY

DL 045 CD2-98

次の（　　）内に、与えられた文字で始まる適切な語を１語ずついれ、音声を聞いて確認しましょう。

A man and his wife were early for a dinner ①(a　　　　　) at a friend's home one night, so they stopped in an ②(e　　　　　) café to have a drink. At the café, the man happened to come across a very ③(f　　　　　) jazz musician there.

After getting the musician's ④(b　　　　　) card, the man and his wife went to dinner. His friends were ⑤(a　　　　　) that he had met such a famous person.

Later that night, the man could not fall asleep because he was too excited about what had happened. He got a shock when he looked the musician up on the ⑥(I　　　　　). The man he had met was an ⑦(i　　　　　).

Several months later, he ran into the "musician" again at a hotel ⑧(b　　) in Greenwich Village. He decided to go to the elderly man's table. However, when he saw ⑨(a　　　　　) in the elderly man's eyes, he came to realize that the sad, old man was not dangerous, but probably just suffering from ⑩(l　　　　　).

DIALOGUE

🎧 DL 046 💿 CD2-99

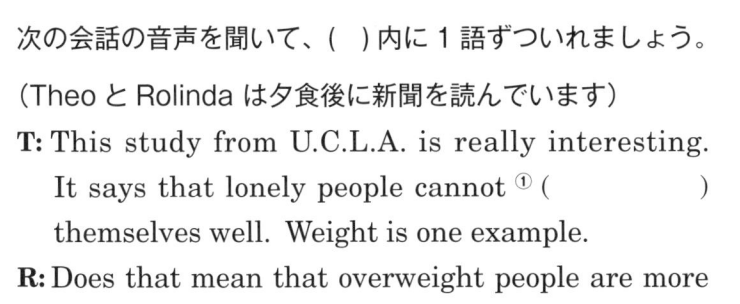

次の会話の音声を聞いて、( ) 内に1語ずついれましょう。

(Theo と Rolinda は夕食後に新聞を読んでいます)

T: This study from U.C.L.A. is really interesting. It says that lonely people cannot ① (　　　　) themselves well. Weight is one example.

R: Does that mean that overweight people are more likely to be lonely?

T: I'm not sure, but according to the study, lonely people ② (　　　　) ③ (　　　　) ④ (　　　　) anything they can to make themselves feel better. Often this means overeating, drinking too much, smoking, or engaging in bad habits.

R: So, it is a ⑤ (　　　　) or mental problem, right?

T: Umm… no, even if they do not have this lack of control, loneliness can raise stress hormone levels and inflammation. The damage affects every system in the body.

R: So such a person is more likely to have a ⑥ (　　　　) ⑦ (　　　　)?

T: Yes, and other diseases. A lonely person reacts more strongly to negative events. This makes his or her ⑧ (　　　　) ⑨ (　　　　) weaker.

R: So they get colds and become sick more easily than people who are social. Whew. I am glad that I have you, Theo. I never feel lonely with you around.

Notes ▸ U.C.L.A = University of California at Los Angeles　be likely to ~「~の可能性が強い」　inflammation「(感情などの) 燃え上がり」　immune system「免疫システム (生体が異質の物質・細胞・組織から体を防衛するために体内に存在する免疫反応発生システム)」

✳ COMPREHENSION

上の Dialogue の内容に関する質問の答えとして適切なものを a ~ c から選びましょう。

1. Which is **not** true about loneliness, according to the story?
   a. It seems that lonely people are more likely to catch a cold.
   b. It seems that lonely people are more likely to suffer heart attacks.
   c. It seems that lonely people exercise more than social people.

2. What seems to be at the root of the problem for lonely people?
   a. They are frightened of cancer due to their increased smoking levels.
   b. They are less able to regulate their behavior in daily life.
   c. Early dementia makes them forget that they have other problems.

Unit 15 Battling the Blues　91

VOCABULARY BUILDING

A　次の太字の語が同じ対比を表すように、空欄に入る適切な語をa～cから選びましょう。

1. **Compliment** is to _____ as **quit** is to **begin**.
    a. behavior　　　　　b. praise　　　　　c. insult
2. **Kindergarten** is to **German** as **café** is to _____.
    a. Italian　　　　　b. French　　　　　c. Spanish
3. **Number** is to **song** as **brave** is to _____.
    a. courageous　　　b. afraid　　　　　c. action
4. _____ is to **smile** as **sob** is to **cry**.
    a. smirk　　　　　b. chuckle　　　　c. grin
5. **Luxurious** is to **elegant** as _____ is to **dangerous**.
    a. perilous　　　　b. rapid　　　　　c. harmless

B　次のそれぞれの文ではgoodが2度使われていますからあまりよい文とはいえません。下線のgoodを言い換えることによって、意味がより明確になります。最も適切な語(句)をa～cから選びましょう。

1. This is a good restaurant, but I wonder if these olives are still good? They taste odd.
    a. safe to eat　　　b. loving　　　　　c. superior in quality
2. This is a good amount of money, but look at the date on this check; I don't think it is good.
    a. valid　　　　　b. kind　　　　　　c. unspoiled
3. I am good at exercising, but I am tired of walking a good two miles to school every day.
    a. enjoyable　　　b. skillful　　　　　c. full
4. Your dad is not only a good father, but he is a lawyer with a good reputation.
    a. helpful　　　　b. honorable　　　　c. well-behaved
5. Your daughter is good at drawing and she has such good manners as well!
    a. skillful　　　　b. beneficial　　　　c. proper

本書には音声CD（別売）があります

Reading Wonders
Food for Thought and Communication
英語で読み、感じ、考えるための15章

2015年1月20日	初版第1刷発行
2022年2月20日	初版第7刷発行

著 者　Robert Juppe
　　　　馬　場　幸　雄

発行者　福　岡　正　人
発行所　株式会社　金 星 堂
〒 101-0051　東京都千代田区神田神保町 3-21
Tel.　(03) 3263-3828（営業部）
　　　(03) 3263-3997（編集部）
Fax　(03) 3263-0716
http://www.kinsei-do.co.jp

編集担当／芦川正宏　　　　　　　　　Printed in Japan
印刷・製本所／倉敷印刷株式会社
本書の無断複製・複写は著作権法上での例外を除き禁じられています。
本書を代行業者等の第三者に依頼してスキャンやデジタル化することは、
たとえ個人や家庭内での利用であっても認められておりません。
落丁・乱丁本はお取り替えいたします。

ISBN978-4-7647-3999-4　　C1082